Dearest Whitney,

This book was written by a good friend of ours and we hope that it inspires you achieve greater things in your life in your continuous pursuit of love + happiness.

We are so proud of your achievements so far, and we cannot wait to be a big part of your future success.

Lots of love, luck and success. Dad
XXX.

BREAK◆AWAY

DISCOVER YOUR ULTIMATE CAREER
THROUGH THE JOURNEY OF A LIFETIME

JEREMY BEHRMANN

Dearest Whits,
Really looking forward to
seeing you soon.
Enjoy your parcel. Lots of Love
Neets

Quickfox

Quickfox Publishing
PO Box 12028, Mill Street, 8010,
Cape Town, South Africa

BREAKAWAY

ISBN 978-0-620-63636-0

First edition 2014

Copyright © 2012 Jeremy Behrmann

jeremy@timetobreakaway.com
www.elixirgroup.co.za

Edited by Michelle Bristol Bovey-Wood
Proofread by Claire Behrmann, Emma Thelwell, Ann Crotty,
Penny Mckerron and Georgia Schumann
Cover and book design by Vanessa Wilson

Dear Hilton & Nita

Thank you so much for all your support!
Enjoy the Breakaway
All the best
Jeremy

Not all who wander are lost!
J.R.R. Tolkien

I dedicate this book to my family,
all the loved ones who walk this journey
with me and to the spirit that binds us.

TABLE OF CONTENTS

	Introduction	Location	Breakaway to ...	Practical Tools	Pg. No.
	How to use this book				11
	Introduction				12
1	Awakening	South Africa	Navigate change	Change Readiness	18
2	Cradle of Humankind	Sub-Saharan Highveld	Rise above survival & conformity	Career Constel- lation	26
3	End of the world	Patagonia	Embrace meaning & autonomy		36
4	Vision quest	Europe	Enjoy rite of passage		47
5	Calling	Chile	Discover your vocation		61
6	Blank canvas	Karoo Desert	Discover innovative ideas		74
7	El Dorado	Colombia	Embrace exploration and entrepreneurship	Vocational Dashboard	91

	Introduction	Location	Breakaway to ...	Practical Tools	Pg. No.
8	Survival of the fittest	Galapagos Islands	Face reality, gain experience and complete research	Research Cascade	104
9	Slumdog professionals	Brazil	Optimise education and learn key skills		133
10	The Terminator	Hollywood	Be ahead of the technological curve		145
11	Kidnapped	El Salvador	Learn to play	Breakaway Launchpad	154
12	The butterfly	Ecuador	Embrace renewal		169
13	21st century nomad	Australia	Find balance		178
Breakaway compass					196
14	The core	Indonesia	Explore the unconscious	Breakaway compass	209
15	The blind spot	Plettenberg Bay, South Africa	Uncover the trauma		219
16	Ayuhuasca	Colombia	Access the supernatural		226
17	Full circle	South Africa	Embrace your ultimate purpose		236

HOW TO USE THIS BOOK

The piloting of this book demonstrated that people gained more value when they read through the whole book, as well as the practical exercises and then returned to complete the exercises at the end.

At the end of each chapter, there is a QR code which, when scanned, will take you to photographs, resources and templates relevant to each chapter.

It is very important that you treat the practical section as a live and organic process that will evolve over time. Do not worry if you do not have all the answers now. You often have to build a wall with ugly bricks in order to eventually hang your crystal chandelier.

INTRODUCTION

Breakaway tells the story of a vocational quest that changed my life forever. I hope that my experiences will offer a compass to help you navigate your own personal journey in the quest to discovering your vocation.

Two forces prompted me to embark on the journey that led to this book. Firstly, I had reached a crossroads in my life where, for some unknown reason, I was unhappy in what I thought would be my dream career, and I felt compelled to throw myself into the void that would inevitably bring me to a place of greater contentment and fulfilment. Once I had made the leap on nothing more than a primal intuition, a huge part of my experience became about understanding why I had made the choice to do so.

It was the best decision I ever made. My journey reinforced that not only was I in the right career, but it also provided me with the opportunity to discover key innovations that would be critical to my success in the industry.

The second reason that I "set sail" on my own personal rite of passage was to address another recurring issue that I kept encountering during my work as a career and entrepreneurship coach. In a world in which we have never had greater choice, more access to information, or a greater level of freedom to develop meaningful and lucrative careers, an ever-increasing number of people struggle to know what to do with their lives. When coming to terms with the fact that we are not happy and when our original expectations or plans do not come to fruition, or when faced with key transitions, such as graduation or retirement, why do so many of us simply feel stuck, or make impulsive decisions?

To try to understand the answers to this question, I engaged in what is essentially a study of the 21st century career landscape – and I discovered that the map many of us have been given does not represent the realities of the professional or vocational landscape with which we are currently faced. Something has changed.

We live in a turbulent age in which there are now literally tens of thousands of different career options that are changing all of the time. The concept of having one job for life is most definitely outdated, and products become irrelevant as quickly as they find popularity. Expensive, time-consuming degrees no longer guarantee jobs. Statistics around business failure and personal debt are alarming. Yet still, in the midst of a recession, people hold out for their ideal jobs, or to dreams of starting innovative, successful businesses.

This terrain is going to change even further, thanks to tectonic shifts in technology, which influence the way in which we develop careers and design our lives.

Herein lies the challenge of modern-day career development and the real essence of a Breakaway: if you want to discover a meaningful and innovative career that reflects your unique combination of passions, values and abilities, there is no map. You have to create and navigate your own, personal journey. It is for this reason that I describe Breakaway as a compass: ultimately, the landmarks of convention are clouded and obscured and you need to be able to map your own way with a greater degree of freedom, while developing the most critical skill needed in the jungle of 21st century career development – adaptation.

I have also learned that the conventional education systems that are meant to open us up to opportunity and prepare us for the future can potentially be the very things that close us off and limit our versatility.

Consider the following: in most major developed economies, we are required at the age of 16 to choose certain educational subjects while disregarding others. Two years later, we are told to decide what we want to study at tertiary level. We need to make these decisions with usually no more than a week of work experience, or our own personal assumptions, to guide us. Most of these decisions, like a lot of what we learn at school, were theoretical and influenced by the people who cared about us, but who ultimately did not have a good understanding and appreciation of our ultimate destinies.

Besides the significant levels of debt that we accumulate by studying for traditional degrees, massive competition for vacancies means that degrees now need to be targeted towards specific careers. If we are lucky enough to end up working in jobs in our chosen fields, we often find ourselves drowning in debt caused by credit cards, bonds and other trappings of life. This makes it even more difficult to find the professional or financial space to explore any different career options.

Breakaway seeks to overcome the massive convergence of perspective and the standardisation of potential experienced in your youth in order to provide a valuable window in which to explore, reflect, conceptualise and ultimately discover your most exciting career, based on wisdom that comes from direct, personal experience.

Conventionally called gap years or sabbaticals and often viewed as luxuries, these windows of experience have become critical vocational gateways to discovering our most powerful drivers and talents. They are also opportunities to develop self-awareness, discover key innovations and enhance emotional resilience, all invaluable commodities in this day and age. They also provide a once-in-a life-time chance for adventure and fun while enjoying the essence of a real-life journey.

Breakaways are as much a shift in mindset as they are an extraction from your normal environment. Therefore, they are not travel-dependent, yet this book will demonstrate the awesome value that one can enjoy from travel in terms of innovative ideas, character development and sheer life experience. No matter your stage in life or how limited you feel your financial and time constraints to be, this book will create the window of experience that you will need in order to explore and effectively implement a new vocation.

So, let's talk about the three layers of this book. First, there is our journey, then there is my journey and, most importantly, there is your journey.

When I talk about "our journey", I am referring to the collective experience of humanity. I started my Breakaway at the Cradle of Humankind in Africa and followed in the footsteps of our ancestors as they explored and inhabited the rest of the world. Encounters with some of the most fascinating cultures on Earth revealed to me an amazing story about the most powerful influences on our careers and values. None of us are able to make effective choices until we have explored, challenged and satiated what is important to us as individuals.

For generations, many cultures have sent people out into the wilderness or on some rite of passage to learn more about themselves and the world and to receive their vision of their spiritual destiny. Great nations have sent explorers on voyages to discover other parts of the world, with the objective of bringing back new perspectives, innovations and tales of adventure to their societies. This legacy has created a huge desire in us to venture forth, discover, explore, uproot and taste the variety that the world has to offer. In essence, this is what many people are seeking when they go on a Breakaway. By understanding and fully embodying our collective journey, we are essentially enriching our own journeys.

Through the study of human anatomy, mankind has learned to live longer. The most significant early advances in this field were made not through theory, but from actually dissecting, experimenting and observing the human body on the laboratory table. By sharing my journey, I am offering up the body of my experience for dissection for your benefit. My track record as a career coach, who has helped hundreds of clients develop successful careers and businesses, while dedicating years to researching the changing nature of career development, makes me a very healthy specimen for this purpose.

As the scalpel of vulnerability cuts a little deeper, you will unearth all sources of dis-ease that plague your career journey. In my case, I was afflicted by uncertainty, conformity, escape and even addiction. Make no mistake: this is a personal journey.

Breakaways cover far more than just careers, and my experience extends way beyond just coaching. My voyage helped me to appreciate the true nature of my relationships, childhood and life experiences. The organ of career cannot prosper in isolation, and the critical areas of family, spirituality, physical health and even intimacy, all impact on our ability to achieve what I believe this book to be about: fulfilment.

This book will help you on your journey by guiding you through a practical coaching process. I believe that Breakaways are about embracing one of life's great paradoxes: control and complete powerlessness. Through innovative coaching tools, such as the Career Constellation; Vocational Dashboard; Research Cascade; and the Launchpad, you can design an experience that helps you to explore your most exciting vocational opportunities based on current awareness.

These tools also make critical provision for time to complete your exploration, without prescribing any agenda or idea of where you may end up. As you make surprise discoveries on your trip, the Breakaway Compass will help you refine your plan along your journey to your ultimate vocation. You get to choose your own adventure.

Bon voyage!

AWAKENING

The hospital hallway was dark, empty and sterile. Perching in a leather chair that did little to ease my discomfort, I braced myself for the inevitable blow that I feared would bring my world crashing down. The hospital environment was completely silent, yet my mind clanged like the bell of an emergency room while doctors debated the consequences of losing an organ that was critical to the body of our family. The organ was my father.

He had been fighting cancer for 17 years, most of my life. Months before his death, I had been called back from university by my father to attend a meeting with the whole family. Had I known when I was called into his room that I would be having my last conscious conversation with the man who had been the dominant force and inspiration in my life, I would have chosen my words better.

The past 10 years of his life had been a consistent and confusing cycle of chemotherapy, radiation treatment and regression, leading to the inevitable return of the cancer. Through all of this, he had made senior partner of his law firm and had been voted one of the top 100 global lawyers by the prestigious Chambers and Partners. His sheer strength of mind and character allowed a naive adolescent respite from dealing with the gravity of his condition.

When we walked into his room, he was sitting up against the headboard of the hospital bed; trying to carry himself in the same manner he would enter his many meetings with executives. Despite his fear, he managed to maintain an air of emotional detachment so that he could get down to the agenda at hand – introducing the trust that would manage the wealth he had spent most of his life amassing. It had afforded him a comfortable retirement that he would never get to enjoy.

Like the law, which had distracted him from the ravages of cancer for many years, the discussion around finances allowed my father to avoid his emotions. To my father, money was always a means of control.

Once the words that summed up his financial legacy had been spoken, their importance in the grand scheme of things began to drift into insignificance. There was no question that his persistence in life had created opportunities for his family that many can only dream of, yet in his eyes I still saw a longing for something more.

That day, in that room, at the age of 64, was the first time I had ever seen my father cry and reveal a vulnerability that I, as a young man, had on many levels craved to see. Still, he did his best to reassure us that he did not fear death and that we would all be alright. The expression on his face told me a very different story.

Deep in his blue eyes, watery from tears long overdue, I saw a wish that we had spent more time together. There was so much that I wanted to share with him. I have no doubt that he had wanted to guide me through many of life's trials, which make fatherhood such a precious gift. Given that conversation around money, I've always pondered how much, in his final moments, he would have given up just to spend more time with us, and to enjoy the other things that he loved.

On reflection, my father worked unbelievably hard and made sacrifices that children at the tender age of 18 don't always fully understand. That said, my dominant memory from childhood is of my father always being at the office, seldom visiting me at boarding school, and being called away at Christmas time to close an important merger between two companies.

Whether by choice or perceived necessity, my father was a slave to his work. I still wonder whether at the crucial moment – the time when he asked the big question about what his life meant – whether he was happy with the answer. How did he feel when he reflected on the values that had governed his life and the consequences in which they had resulted?

My biggest fear is that my father felt he had no choices. Did the burden of financial responsibility mean that he had no option but to continue working day and night to feed the money machine? Was he compelled by pressure to conform to the expectations of his tribe: the ever-ambitious Jewish community of South Africa, where being a captain of industry or an esteemed professional is often the perceived basis for acceptance?

Could it have been some personal mission borne out of his appreciation and talent for the law that consciously drove him? Or was it the need to prove himself to his father, who had also died before his time?

Perhaps, like many of us, he just suffered from a lack of awareness of what he could do differently to bring his life into greater balance?

While my father was quietly battling cancer and trying to shape our future in the face of his mortality, I became an angry young man during his final years. Besides coming to terms with my own fear and inability to help him during his gradual demise, I was trying to find my own identity through my adolescence. I felt that my father, who was now responding from a place of fear, had never embraced my ideas and had always created opportunities for me based on his value system, without acknowledging my own. But he was also a huge inspiration to me and I often blindly followed in his footsteps to success without fully questioning my own beliefs.

Without any self-awareness of who I was, nor the ability to stand up for my own beliefs, it was easy for my father to use one all-too-familiar tool to control my development: money. The chaotic interplay between my need to find independence and his desire to influence my life filled the last chapter of his life with conflict, anger and confusion. There were words that needed to be said, but his fight with cancer was drawn out over so many years, and the emotional gap between us simply grew until we would just never have that conversation.

I was called back again from university overseas on the news that his cancer had advanced. When I returned, I found that the lucid, dynamic and charming maverick that I remembered suddenly appeared almost infantile, thanks to the high dose of morphine that gave him comfort. As I walked in, his eyes lit up with a mix of delight and fear. He knew that my unexpected return from the United Kingdom could mean only one thing.

Over the next few weeks, he grew weaker and weaker until it was no longer possible to speak to him. I would just stare at his closed eyes, hoping that they would reopen and afford me one last chance to say goodbye.

While we were standing at his bedside, the nurse informed us that it was almost time, and we braced ourselves for the end. She then turned off the heart rate monitor to save us the torment of hearing his heart come to an audible stop. After a few moments, she checked his vital signs, dipped her head slightly in defeat, and then looked at us with eyes that were well trained at delivering the most devastating of finalities.

The room went quiet, just before it exploded with our tears and emotion. I hugged my stepmother. We had been the only loved ones with him when he passed. Although his condition had been terminal for so long, he had passed away so quickly that the rest of the family, who had been rushing to the hospital, had missed his final moments.

It is impossible for a young person to understand the full implications of losing a father at such a young age. He was our tribe leader, and as we consoled each other in the face of our loss, I was numb to the shock and confusion of the massive blow that had just struck me. My world would spiral out of control for a number of years before I fully understood the impact my father's death had on my life.

After his death, besides the expressions of gratitude and requests for forgiveness that I could only direct at him through prayer, something shifted inside me. Perhaps it was disillusionment, a profound questioning, or simply an inability to let things go.

The experience of losing my father gave rise to a deep need to understand the experiences that had shaped his life and what had influenced the choices he had made. The pain caused by his passing, and the anger that I felt at having been denied his presence in my life, created what I now understand to be a healthy questioning of the system in which my father operated. Why did he not make the changes that were so easily within his reach? What forces led him to believe that his approach to life was exactly what he wanted for the rest of his days? Did he miss out on an opportunity to discover something new? Would he have grabbed it with both hands?

I believe that a Breakaway was really what my father needed – and very much what he deserved. It would have given him the space to reflect upon his life; the opportunity to experiment with other ways of living; to conceptualise different ways in which he could approach his career; and ultimately to have had experiences that would have challenged or supported the way he lived his life. He would have been afforded the opportunity to just live – to have had an experience just for the sake of having it, without the fear, guilt and pressure that dominates so much of our lives.

So, when I made my way out into the unknown, I realised that I was taking a Breakaway for myself as much as for my father, who never enjoyed the opportunity. It would be a gateway to discovering who I was and to understanding more about who he was, too. The question was: Where to start?

Your turn – Change readiness

Change is inevitable, yet we don't always fully grasp the degree to which we are changing, or how quickly the world around us is evolving. The catalyst that sparks a Breakaway may be a formal, expected life event, such as coming to the end of your schooling, university or professional career and being unsure of which direction you should take, or it may be completely unexpected. You may suddenly find yourself questioning your passion for your career or witnessing your product becoming irrelevant in the marketplace. Perhaps you were even fired from your job.

Part of growing up is learning that as we mature and change, we have to continually tune our compass to give us more accurate readings in new stages of our lives. In times of serious change, the skies around us can seem very murky and grey and the landmarks of conventional life that make us feel safe and secure are not necessarily visible to us.

Face up to change

When it comes to facing change, the biggest mistake we can make is to go into denial. Some of us continue through life in complete unconsciousness, driven by our attachment to our beliefs, goals, positions and even possessions. But these "things" may not reflect the true essence of our changing values and where we find ourselves in our lives.

The second big mistake is to accept that something is changing, yet not do anything about it. Albert Einstein describes insanity as doing the same thing over and over again and expecting a different result. Many of us wake up hoping that today will be different, yet change nothing about our approach to life. People choose to escape their reality in different ways, such as taking medication or by rebelling against their lives and the change they are experiencing. They want the status quo to remain.

When we know we are living without inner integrity, yet fail to do anything about it because of fear, shame or an attachment to the way things have always been done, an inner volcano is created. If we don't take responsibility for our deepest needs, regret, stress and even resentment can well up inside of us until we feel like we are about to explode.

Many of us tend to view change as an obstacle rather than an opportunity. History has shown that during every recession, successful businesses have been founded by people who have, by force of circumstance, navigated themselves into more fulfilling careers. When George Lucas was 18 years old, he was determined to be a racing car driver. That year, he was involved in a disastrous racing accident that shattered his expectations. He went on to create *Star Wars* and *Indiana Jones*, two of the most successful movie franchises in the world.

Walt Disney was sent to France to serve in the war. As an ambulance driver, he saw the most horrifying atrocities, but that pain and suffering evoked a deep desire to create different pictures of reality. He returned to America to train as an animator and a cartoonist.

In times of change, it is easy to blame others or to become a victim of your circumstances, rather than facing the fact that life is full of surprises and you don't always know what is best for you in every situation. Irrespective of how you view change, the ability to respond, or "responsibility", speaks to how well you accept and adapt to your shifting circumstances. That response may be a conscious decision to do nothing and to continue as you are, or it may require a bold step into the unknown. At least by exploring the manner in which things are changing you can make conscious choices, rather than impulsive decisions or just sticking your head in the sand.

⊕ ACTION

Please answer the following questions and save them in a journal or on a Word document on your computer:

1. What shifts are you experiencing in your life now, or are you expecting to respond to in the short to medium term?

2. What are the dominant feelings that this change has been evoking within you for the past while? Excitement, curiosity, fear? Are you feeling overwhelmed?

3. Looking back, are you surprised that this change is happening? In which areas can you take responsibility for what is transpiring?

4. What will happen if you do not respond to this call for change? What consequences do you foresee?

5. What potential can you move towards as you navigate this change?

THE CRADLE OF HUMANKIND

The cool breeze off the plateau brought welcome respite from the intense African heat as I walked across the grasslands. As I came to rest on arguably the most significant piece of land in recorded human history, the soil was warm underfoot, as if life itself was still being spawned from the bosom of the motherland.

Looking out over the awe-inspiring beauty of the savannah, I could not help but be amazed that a visit to this place was not a significant rite of passage for all of humanity.

A package had arrived for me a few weeks before. It contained a map from one of the most prestigious institutions in the world: the National Geographic Society. But this was no ordinary map. The way it had been created was as fascinating as the journey it depicted.

Months before, I had received a DNA tool kit that required me to swab the inside of my mouth and then return the sample to Washington DC for scrutiny. Genetic researchers at the Genographic Project have identified 150 000 different "markers", which are like tracks that show the various journeys made by our ancestors as they populated the Earth.

Every individual has a unique combination of markers, so I was provided with an exact map that showed the specific journey of my own bloodline. What was also really interesting, although not a shock to my girlfriend, was that 3% of my make-up was Neanderthal.

I knew that my father's ancestors were from Lithuania, so it was not a huge surprise that my dominant ancestral group came from Bulgaria and Romania. What became more apparent as I followed the trail further back in time was that the path of my ancestors started in Africa, from where *Homo sapiens* emerged. In fact, all of ours did!

In the South African province of Gauteng lies what is called the Cradle of Humankind, the site of arguably the most important archaeological discovery in the world. This unique site has provided humanity with its greatest understanding of where life began. The area has yielded more than 35% of the world's early hominid fossils and is also home to the earliest discovered fossilised evidence of a living organism, and the oldest recorded use of fire and tools by humans.

For God-fearing people around the world, visits to the religious epicentres of Jerusalem, St Peter's Basilica and Mecca are the culmination of meaningful journeys that pilgrims hope will answer or reinforce the fundamental question: WHY? Why are we here? Why does life exist?

Feeling like an explorer seeking the Holy Grail of self-awareness, it made sense that I start my Breakaway here, where the trail began. Man's journey started in Africa, and I was excited about what I would discover about myself from visiting this nursery of humanity and retracing our steps.

So, why did life first spring up in Africa?

Next to the town of Vredefort, about 200km south of the Cradle of Humankind, is a dome indicating the area where a 10km-wide meteor collided with the Earth's crust at 100 000km per hour. The resulting explosion had the power of 10 million atomic bombs. It left a crater 300km wide that can still be seen from space.[1]

Unlike many "Armageddon" meteorites that are believed to have killed off much of life on this planet, this explosion was responsible for accelerating creation.

It is believed that before the Vredefort meteor hit the planet more than two billion years ago, Earth's surface comprised mainly rock, water and gases, supporting only basic life forms that could survive in an oxygen-starved, noxious atmosphere. The meteor punctured Earth's crust, releasing significant amounts of oxygen into the atmosphere, prompting more complex life forms to emerge. These first evolved in the area closest to the source of the explosion: the South African highveld.

Standing in the exhibition space close to the Sterkfontein Caves, the home of many of the archaeological discoveries on the site, I stared deep into the dark voids that would have been the eyes of Mrs Ples, an ancient skeleton that we now consider to be the missing link between homo sapiens and apes. Mrs Ples's mouth was agape, as if releasing a haunting scream across the display area. I saw in her "face" the harsh realities of life at a time when she could expect to survive to the ripe age of 18 – the legal drinking age in most countries.

The challenges facing early humans were enormous. When they weren't being hunted by predators or competing against other early hominid species for shelter, they would have been scavenging carcasses.

---

[1] *Fieldguide to the Cradle of Humankind*, Prof. Lee R. Berger and Brett Hilton-Barber, Struik, 2002

They travelled in groups comprising too few people to overpower even the smallest and weakest of animals. They continued this perilous existence until, in a moment of sheer inspiration, they formed arguably the most influential organisational structure in humanity's history: the tribe.

To enhance our ability to reproduce – the most important driver of all animals – we had to develop alliances. The ability to reproduce is made easier if you can rely on the support of friends and relations. Our ability to develop and maintain these complex social alliances provided a quantum leap in analytical skills, foresight and reason.[2] Thanks to the tribe, each individual was safer and afforded the entire group's protection from other predators or from other homo species that were still scavenging or hunting in smaller groups. They could finally hunt in packs, which significantly improved their success rate in securing food. The new-found efficiency of the clan in providing the basic elements of survival freed up energy and time. Man's physiology responded to these new circumstances by producing more oxytocin, the brain chemical that allows us to bond more effectively with our new tribe members and build trust, which is the key to alliances. It's as if our genes learned that the human bonding required to create and maintain these new tribes would increase our chances of survival. To be rejected by the tribe meant almost certain death.[3]

Tribe members educated people about their history by telling stories around the fire that were passed down from generation to generation. This oral story-telling tradition was regarded as sacred. It

---

[2]   http://www.nature.com/nature/journal/v435/n7042/abs/nature03701.html (accessed 4/10/2014)

[3]   *Fieldguide to the Cradle of Humankind*, Prof. Lee R. Berger and Brett Hilton-Barber, Struik, 2002

ensured that the tribe's beliefs and way of living were protected, securing the livelihood of the tribe itself.[4]

The power of the tribe

On one level or another, all of our Breakaways seek to explore possible answers to the reasons for our existence. We essentially hope to gain a greater appreciation for why we are alive, and to give meaning to our lives.

On a Breakaway, we are on a journey to discover who we are, what makes us tick, and what influences our decisions. It is possible to forget that our journey as individuals started way before we were even born. From the moment that we come into this world, our consciousness is expressed through our genes, which already carry a map and history of our evolution dating back billions of years. We carry the DNA of the tribe within us.

Think for a moment about the tribes that are exerting influence over you right now, and those that have impacted on your past decisions. Even though there are no sabre-tooth tigers patrolling your environment, which would make expulsion from your tribe potentially deadly, our need to be accepted by our tribes is still very real. It influences the way we behave, our belief systems, the clothes we buy, the music we listen to, and the careers and life paths that we consider respectable.

When we are young, our families or schools are our tribes. Parents, like teachers, are the tribal leaders. They represent safety, structure, security and survival in an unknown world. Besides passing on all of the practical knowledge that helps us to effectively survive in the world,

---

[4]   *Origins Reconsidered*, Richard Leakey and Roger Lewin, Little Brown,1992

they also pass on their own values, beliefs and fears to us, the next generation.

I remember sitting around the dinner table while my family entertained guests, unaware that my brain, like a sponge, was taking in every detail, as if it was the gospel coming from on-high. Irrespective of whether the conversation was gossip, nonsense, speculation or legend, my brain was masterfully placing patterns together that would eventually draw a concrete picture of the world. In reality, I was desperately seeking to understand the expectations of my tribe, so I could learn them and, in so doing, gain acceptance.

Like the stories around the tribal fire, many of the principles that would be passed down to me were for my own protection and the maintenance of society as we know it. Other principles were purely subjective – the perspectives of people who were trying to come to terms with a world that they too, did not understand.

When I looked into the "eyes" of Mrs Ples, I saw myself as a young child, fully reliant on my parents to meet my needs. My parents maintained order through discipline and whenever I stepped out of line, I was corrected either with a good spanking or a stern talking to. As I grew older, the mechanism of discipline became financial. I would push the boundaries as far as I could, but each time, the fear of being cut off financially and banished to the wilderness on my own brought me back into line.

When we think of the various Breakaways with which we would like to engage, the age-old social practices of the tribe become evident. Some tribal leaders don't want their young to leave the tribe as they are fearful of losing them forever. Some parents would rather their children "played small" at home than "played big" elsewhere. Other parents are concerned that the world is filled with uncertainty and that it is too risky to take unknown paths.

Other parent-leaders take pride in their own paths to success and regard their offspring going in a different direction as a betrayal of trust, respect and tribal values. As a result, when it comes to choosing a career or life path, these leaders often only provide their children with guidance based on their own views or beliefs, whether they be financial or emotional.

Some parents remain truly open to letting their young ones discover things for themselves, yet their children still follow in their footsteps. With limited self-awareness around their own values, passions and abilities, these children often just take on the values of the people they love and respect the most. This could be the parent – or even the most popular boy at school.

Breakaways involve risk

Choosing to defy or go against our tribal leaders and take a Breakaway journey is a risk. It means leaving the safety of the tribe, a secure income and the certainty that comes with familiar customs, traditions and routines. Stepping out of our comfort zone brings up the most primal of fears that we have inherited from our ancestors, namely abandonment, starvation, rejection, and a fear of being lost.

In the 21st century, the likelihood of facing the same challenges as the people who inhabited the area around the Cradle of Humankind is highly unlikely, yet the feelings and fears we experience are exactly the same.

Many of you reading this book could have been in your careers for some time and may even feel that you are the tribal leaders. Your family, colleagues or friends rely on you for safety, prosperity, guidance and emotional support. The very notion of going on a Breakaway to explore a new vocation that may fulfill you may seem unrealistic, irresponsible and perhaps just too risky.

You can only be a good parent, partner or employee if you are happy with what you are doing. Living out of integrity with one's values can only lead to stress, burnout and even resentment of the very people for whom you are making the sacrifice. What's more, a Breakaway can open your eyes to different ways in which you can design your life while creating the freedom for your whole family to discover new things about themselves, and ways in which they can contribute to the family or relationship dynamic. As you will discover, Breakaways can be a quantum leap forward in your professional development and should not be seen as a step backwards.

Little has changed over the ages

In and around the Sterkfontein Caves – the site of the oldest evidence of our ability to create fire – I observed massive holes in the ground where tombs filled with fascinating artefacts revealed our collective ancestry. I took out my smartphone and compared this advanced electronic device to a rough and jagged piece of stone that had been shaped into a knife hundreds of thousands of years before. I took a photo and uploaded it to Facebook.

Nowadays, we like to pretend that we are far more advanced than our archaic ancestors. However, social media like Facebook does nothing more than replicate the basic dynamics of the tribe on a global scale. This particular site was originally created to facilitate the most primal of needs: to know who was single and to evaluate their status (read: mating potential) on the Harvard University campus.

Through newsfeeds, we hope to stay abreast of the trends and movements of our tribe, constantly doing our best to stay fulfilled (survive) in this fast-paced social ecosystem that feeds us with more ideas, expectations and beliefs about the way that the world works. We update our profiles with personal information in the hope that we will be liked (accepted) by an ever larger network of tribe members, thus providing us with safety.

The reality is that we are still influenced by our primal nature. At the core of the Breakaway is the creation of the space needed to explore these aspects of our nature and to decide for ourselves what beliefs and values govern our life. Free from the influence of our peers, parents and the conventional norms of our community at home, a Breakaway allows us to discover things for ourselves.

Painting your own canvas

The Cradle of Humankind was fascinating. It told me the first chapter of humanity's story, but what I really wished to see were the footprints of that first person who overcame their instincts and primal fears and left the safety of his or her tribe to explore the unknown. Millions of years down the line, where would this genetic trail end? What stories would that early pioneer have to share?

The footprints that I sought had been buried in the sands of time. What remained was a blank canvas of sand stretching out before me at the start of my own journey. I realised that by perhaps throwing caution to the wind and exploring what was over the horizon, I could understand why I was ready to leave everything behind to Breakaway.

Your turn – Exploring values

It is vital that you understand your values. They are the compass that must guide your Breakaway and ultimately, your life's journey. That said, a Breakaway is also designed to expose you to other ways of living your life and most importantly to challenge your values to make sure they are your own.

Your desire to step out of your comfort zone to explore the world goes very much against the need for certainty, safety and financial security. As you discover new values that make you feel independent and unique, they could conflict with those of others, like your parents, who raised you with their unique set of values. Your parents may view a "gap year" as a complete waste of time. Or perhaps your partner thinks that a sabbatical, or Breakaway, is a financial risk because you are planning to have children in a few years' time.

What you need to appreciate is that no matter how sophisticated your values may be, they are still based on a set of fundamental needs that we all share. These values can be as basic as food and water, or as complex as the desire for global harmony. The key lies in understanding what your values are, where they come from, and how to resolve conflicts – both in yourself and others. This will clear the way for your Breakaway.

🌐 ACTION

Please answer the following questions and save them in a journal or on a Word document on your computer:

1. What key expectations have you created for your life? What goals, targets or symbols determine success in your mind?
2. Which of these come from your parents or esteemed peers?
3. Which values can you say are truly your own?
4. Where do you feel you have violated your own values to gain acceptance?
5. In what ways have you not opened yourself up to change to feel certain of your survival?

3

THE END OF THE WORLD

PATAGONIA

Nowadays, there are very few places where one can experience absolute freedom: a space free from distractions, pollution, pressure and all of the other trappings of our modern age. It is rare to find an environment so foreign that who you are – as defined by where you come from, what you do for a living, who your friends are, what masks you wear, the insecurities you carry, and the baggage of life – fall away. For me, Patagonia is such a place.

I started my journey in Santiago, the Chilean capital. It took two flights, an eight-hour drive, a half-morning sail across a lake and a horseback ride to reach a ranch in the heart of the mountains. It was an epic journey in itself.

There, in one of the least populated places on Earth, I had no cellphone reception or internet – nothing that would distract me from being completely in the present. My phone's keypad was replaced by a journal, and television made way for the most beautiful vistas I have ever seen.

Standing on the edge of massive cliffs, I observed the awesome ice fields bordering Chile and Argentina. The glaciers, like colossal arms, steadily stretched out into the ocean, displaying nature's patient conviction.

I was brought almost to tears as I contemplated the meaning of my life in the midst of such natural beauty. All of the confusion and fear that I had felt in the run-up to my Breakaway was replaced by a razor-sharp sense of clarity and confidence. I knew what I needed to do in order to live a life of authenticity, integrity and ultimately, balance.

I reflected on my values outside of the conditioning that had governed my thinking at home and at work. I was no longer subject to the beliefs of my family and friends. Finally, I had the space and freedom to really emerge as myself.

I found the people of Patagonia to be as rugged as the windswept plains. They have carved out an existence for themselves in the harshest of conditions. It is a place of cowboys, criminals on the run, and farmers who eke a living working the hardest of lands.

During one particular horse ride, we arrived at a smallholding on the edge of a massive glacial lake near the Andes-Argentine frontier. We were greeted by a traditional gaucho (Argentinian cowboy) named Lorenzo. As is customary, we only dismounted our horses on his invitation. He then directed us towards the entrance of his house.

Lorenzo was a short man with a self-confidence that spoke of an ability to survive in the most dangerous of environments. His family kept chickens, hunting dogs, horses and some oxen. They had no electricity other than a small solar panel that powered a radio. The purpose of the communication was to check in with his neighbours who lived miles apart. Instead, they gossiped about each other, hoping it would spark a conflict that would provide hours of excitement.

Inside the house, we met Lorenzo's wife, who was barely 5ft tall. The couple had lived on the smallholding all of their lives. There was no television, books or any other form of visible entertainment. The expression on his wife's face suggested that the novelty of solitude in the wilderness had passed some time before.

As is customary, we were presented with a cup of mate, a herb grown in the Argentine that is drunk by locals throughout the day – another form of procrastination. (So cherished is the brew, that in one of the region's biggest villages, Coyhaique, there is a statue of a hand breaking through the ground, grasping at a cup of the precious tea in a moment of defiance against all things industrious.) Every night Lorenzo would prepare a pot of mate and a fire and leave his front door open, offering solace and shelter to anyone crossing the border.

After the mate ceremony, Lorenzo revealed what would be the highlight of the entertainment: a bottle containing a clear liquid. The label indicated it contained 80% alcohol. In the interests of maintaining South African-Patagonian relations, I declined and instead opted for some traditional bread, or "pan", accompanied by prune jam made by his wife.

Although my Spanish was weak, I tried to convey my appreciation to Lorenzo's wife through body language. It may have been lost in translation as some form of flirtation, for every time I looked around the room, she was staring at me as if I was a piece of fresh meat. I suspected that anything with a heartbeat would be fair game in this part of the world.

Staring up at the ceiling to avoid eye contact with the Argentinian cougar, I noted bullet holes in the walls. I made no mention of this in case it provoked some form of demonstration with a rusty pistol. On the way home that night, I would learn their origin from a relative.

Lorenzo's mother had died without a will, so the land had undergone a succession process in which the government owned the property until an agreement between the successors had been reached. The bullet holes were the culmination of a failed negotiation between Lorenzo and his younger siblings. Perhaps the traditional alcohol had proved to be an ineffective ice-breaker on that occasion.

As we left the house, Lorenzo's wife presented me with a jar of jam, much to the delight of my relatives who had also noted the advances of the Patagonian battle-axe. We took photographs with the couple, mounted our horses and then left them to their own devices in that cold, remote valley in the heart of the Patagonia.

Reflecting on the warm plains of Africa, I wondered how our early ancestors could leave the temperate sub-Saharan region to explore an icy, unknown world, evade new predators and adapt to the demands of a new environment that could prove lethal to any unprepared inhabitant.

* * *

Patagonia's significance lies in the fact that it is the last place in which humans settled after making the decision to leave the safety of the first tribal family in Africa. Over thousands of years, small groups of people spread throughout Africa, Asia and Europe, across the chain of islands in the Pacific, and into Australia. After various ice ages abated, a small pocket of people crossed the Bering land bridge that links Siberia and Alaska and migrated down through North and South America, until they finally settled in what is now known as Patagonia.[5]

---

[5]   Human Genographic Project, https://genographic.nationalgeographic.com/ (accessed 29/10/2014)

Humanity left Africa 60 000 years ago. Patagonia was settled only 40 000 years later. Why, when the safety of the tribe provided a much stronger guarantee of survival, would a small pocket of people who had, up until that time, thrived on conforming and being accepted by their community, suddenly head off on their own to a remote location like Patagonia?

Imagine your busiest day at work. Your diary is so jam-packed that you have had to use all of your energy and focus just to ensure that you are prepared for a big presentation. You are under such pressure that you do not have the time to reflect on the purpose or meaning of what you are actually doing.

As you walk out of the boardroom after your presentation, you take a breath for the first time and feel your mind relaxing after the intensity of the experience. Suddenly your perspective has returned and you can reflect on what you have achieved and what the experience means.

Imagine now what it was like for our African ancestors who spent all of their time hunting for food, avoiding predators, finding safe places to sleep, fighting off mating rivals and continually responding to the sensory stimuli that provided the information so vital to their survival. Every last bit of energy was consumed by the effort to stay alive. Suddenly, the formation of tribes brought safety in numbers, secure food supplies and a higher probability of mating. They were no longer required to expend all of their energy on survival. Where would this extra energy take them?

For some unknown yet highly spiritual reason, mankind began what would become the greatest search of all: the quest for meaning. Unlike other animals, humans stopped responding purely to physical needs and started exploring who they were and why they were alive.

Instead of merely responding to the cycles of nature, we humans started to question why changes in our environment took place. People began to think more about the mysterious world in which they found themselves, and developed an understanding of the sacred balance of ecology. It is no accident that the first evidence of human spirituality has a deep connection to what we now call nature.

The evidence of this process has been revealed by carbon dating. We know that less than 50 000 years ago, mankind had no art, religion or sophisticated symbolism. Then, in a dramatic and electrifying change, described by scientists as "the greatest riddle in human history", all of the skills and qualities that we value most highly in ourselves appeared to have become fully formed, as though bestowed on us by hidden powers.[6]

A direct result of these newly-acquired skills, the oldest recorded paintings of animal spirits and mystical creatures were found in the depths of caves in South Africa and the Chauvet region of France.[7] The San, the native people of sub-Saharan Africa with the oldest proven homo sapien genetic code to which we are all related, used various dances to induce trance-like hallucinations that allowed them to build relationships with the animal spirits.

Whether our spiritual progression was a result of having more free time and energy, or whether it was influenced by special techniques that allowed early cultures to enter supernatural realms, ultimately the debates around the origins of human spirituality will always be speculative. What cannot be argued is the fact that at some time, humanity began to contemplate not only the meaning of life, but their individual place in it.

---

[6] *Supernatural: Meetings with the Ancient Teachers of Mankind*, Graham Hancock, Paperback, 2006

[7] http://www.bradshawfoundation.com/chauvet/chauvet_cave_paintings.php (accessed 15/05/2013)

The development of the "I"

Just like toddlers who become aware of their own toys for the first time and scream: "Mine!", so too were our early ancestors becoming aware of their own identity in relation to the tribe. It was the first appearance of the "I".

But, finally able to make choices, people started to see the world in different ways. Greater exposure to life beyond the tribe revealed a lack of substance to the superstitions promoted by tribal elders who governed how people thought and behaved: people were not being struck by lightning when they approached the furthest border at full moon; young tribal members were not falling ill when they did not make the correct sacrifices to the sun gods; and the world did not end on completion of an eclipse.

A breakdown in tribal order ensued. Driven by this new freedom, young tribal members sought only to better themselves and to take control of their lives at any cost. Fearing anarchy, tribal leaders layered on more tradition and ritual, stifling those who wanted to break free to find their own autonomy. The horizon no longer represented a place of danger. It came to represent liberation, no matter what perils lay ahead. This is adolescence in its truest essence.

Reaching for the horizon

Arriving in Patagonia as early as 20 000 years ago, the descendants of those who completed the very first Breakaway had crossed the Sahara Desert, navigated thousands of miles of open ocean and survived all manner of natural disasters.

Humanity has been bold in every opportunity to seek a more habitable space in which to live. We have overcome fear in order to break through tribal boundaries and discover our own destinies.

The people of Patagonia embody an explorative and adventurous spirit. They have made their lives so far off the beaten track that they are almost a law unto themselves. However, they still have an appreciation for community.

Riding my horse back to the ranch, I could not help but feel for myself the same admiration that I had for these people. I felt brave for stepping away from my tribe in South Africa and for leaving the security of my family, friends and my business, which had all been central to my financial and emotional stability. Irrespective of any career aspirations I might have had, I had managed a Breakaway. It was not always this way.

* * *

My genes had started punching through my infancy, revealing a young man who wanted to break free to discover his own identity. I was heading straight into that turbulent stage of adolescence in which conforming to the expectations of my family became a distant priority, after rebelling and taking ownership of my individual aspirations.

In my teen years, music grew to be a major passion in my life. My first love was house music, which infused the jazz and disco rhythms my parents enjoyed with the fresher dance beats that I loved. I followed the world's top DJs with the commitment of a disciple, and slowly my love for music developed into an obsession.

Needless to say, our tribe leader, my father, never appreciated my music, or my ambitions to pursue it further. As a youth, I had asked to play the electric guitar or the drums, but my requests had been refused and I was left with the option to play a brass instrument. Only that would satisfy my father's vision of me playing in the high school orchestra.

I chose the flute, but I was not inspired. I ended up playing only concertos selected by our conservative German orchestra leader, and a host of Christmas carols to the family over the festive season.

As fulfilling as it was to make progress on an instrument, the novelty of playing *Hark the Herald Angels Sing* eventually wore off, and I gave up playing the instrument altogether. Instead, I focused on the sounds that really inspired me: electronic music. The way I knew to share this music with people was by becoming a DJ. My father once again refused, saying that it would draw me into the club scene, where he believed that drugs would pose a threat to me.

I was left with no other option but to manipulate the equalisers on my tape deck. Playing with the various levels gave me endless pleasure. I was fascinated by how producers layered various frequencies together to create sounds that could so quickly shift one's emotions.

Huddled next to my hi-fi, I imagined myself rocking with large crowds as the bass line dropped, taking the roof off my living room in the stadium of my mind.

My father never did fully appreciate my passion for electronic music, nor did he provide the resources that I needed to take things further. As a result, during my school years, I would never think of DJing as a potential career.

While my father was stifling my passion for music in what he described as my best interests, he was also fighting off my teachers who begged him to put me on Ritalin.

I had been diagnosed with a form of ADHD and deemed uncontrollable in class because I was always jumping around. What my father did not understand and my teachers never fully appreciated, is that there were things that did engage me. Through the languages of music and the ocean, another passion of mine, I could have been taught anything. I would later discover that I was a kinaesthetic learner, which meant that my dominant desire was to experience the world through movement. The rhythms of the ocean and my ability to dance were the ways in which I wanted to express myself.

Throughout the course of my life, I have understood things and come up with my best ideas while my body was in motion. When I look back on my school days, I understand now that my desire to move around the classroom was my way of thinking. But I was always told to sit down and shut up. At that point, I would usually pick up my pen and start drawing pictures of waves.

As you read this, you may be experiencing a range of emotions. For some of you who are at the end of your school or university days, you may be feeling like one of those young tribal people driven to break free to explore and discover the world for yourself. You may be experiencing anger as you come to terms with the fact that your career choices were influenced by the fears and beliefs of parents who would not let you embrace your own sense of meaning. Perhaps they convinced you that your vision was too risky, that you should get a "real" job or that you should try to be more like your friend Suzanne.

Driven by the need to be certain of your survival, or to be accepted by your family or friends, you may feel that you have now given up on your chance to discover your unique significance. Perhaps you feel a certain sense of regret. It could be that you are even feeling fearful or overwhelmed, as you believe that your dream career or business lies just beyond the horizon. But with risk comes the uncertainty of leaving the tribe for the first time.

We are ultimately driven by an archetypal need to explore our own sense of meaning and to clarify what our lives mean. In the 21st century, this has become not only a trend, but a real need to live a fulfilled life. It calls for a rite of passage in which we take ownership of our passions.

Your turn – Exploring your passions

Your passions are the things that you do simply for the sheer inspiration and meaning they provide to you. We often tend to engage in our passions only when money is not an issue and when we have free time and no responsibilities to anyone other than ourselves. We follow our passions because we love them. It's that simple.

Your Breakaway should afford you the opportunity to turn an interest into a passion and a hobby into a vocation. So, let's start with the most dominant passions – those current and those left by the wayside years ago.

If you are still young and are really struggling to answer these questions – that is exactly why you need a Breakaway. The next chapter will help you take this forward.

ACTION

Please answer the following questions and save them in a journal or on a Word document on your computer:

1. When you have no money, what do you do for fun?
2. When you have money to spare, how do you spend it?
3. If you had one more day to live, how would you spend that day?
4. If you received a voucher to buy 10 books or movies on your favourite subject, what would the topics be?
5. As a child, what did you love doing most?
6. When did you feel closest to your parents?
7. What passions do you consider to be "dying stars"? These are the things that you used to love doing and into which you still plough energy, although they no longer provide the same fulfilment.

VISION QUEST

S taring at the array of knobs, I could not have been more confused. Years of education had left me standing in front of the machine, poking at buttons like a monkey in an experiment. I was 18, doing my first load of washing and feeling lost in London's urban jungle.

My year had been decided for me before I had even left South Africa. With all of the subtlety of a lawyer, my father had persuaded me to attend university overseas. An international education would give me a bit of an insurance policy in case South Africa "started to go the wrong way", he said.

I was in my gap year, and I had eight months in which to find a university, be accepted into an economics degree, and do some travelling. Although I understood how lucky I was to be afforded the opportunity to travel and study overseas, I had not been given much choice in the matter. Nor had I been challenged to think for myself.

Although I had no experience in financial services, I decided to pursue a career in that arena because it gave me the highest probability of being rich. Finance also seemed to be the dominant career aspiration of my peers who, like me, had fathers who were captains of industry.

Instead of heading out into the wilderness on my own to begin discovering who I was, I travelled from London to Europe with two school friends, who were at my side throughout the journey. Our conversations repeatedly echoed familiar jibes and nostalgic stories from our school days, as we continued to play out our predetermined roles in our friendship circle. We had each other, so I had significantly less need to socialise with other people I met on the trip. Although fun, if there had been an opportunity to discover something new about myself or to fully connect with other cultures, it fell away the moment we embarked on our inter-railing trip.

Without any awareness or desire for my trip to have a higher purpose than just travelling to different countries, I behaved like an adolescent liberated from my tribe, out to discover the world for myself through experimentation.

Partying was the common thread that ran through my gap year. These experiences should have been about celebrating life, learning to have fun responsibly, and about exploring our sexuality, different activities, and the cultures of the various countries we visited. But, for me, partying – more specifically drugs and alcohol – became the dominant force that ruled my life, not only through my gap year but into university, too. My substance use accelerated from experimentation into full-blown addiction. My behaviour reflected more of a desire to medicate myself or to escape from something, than a natural process of exploration.

It is vital that people separate themselves from their tribe in order to discover their own sense of authenticity. This is not to say that one must always journey alone, but at least be prepared to enjoy the growth and self-discovery that comes from independent travel. It is critical that one gets to understand one's purpose and feel confident enough to fend for one's self, while developing the skills required to survive and be fulfilled. Over the centuries, cultures have understood this need and have developed all types of rite of passage to facilitate this maturation process. Unfortunately, in my experience and through that of the hundreds of people I interviewed during the development of this book, the rite of passage is being lost – particularly in the Western world.

* * *

Creed medicine man William Walk Sacred had been praying for 18 months in preparation for the most significant rite of passage of his people, the Native American Indians. Although he had been safe and secure in his tribe as an infant, it was finally time for him, as an adolescent, to venture off into the wilderness alone. He was on a journey to discover his manhood and needed to make peace with the creator that had given him life. It was time for his vision quest.[8]

William Walk Sacred's journey was not unique to him: it was one that is undertaken by all young men from his tribe and culture. The Native American Indians believe that we are all on a spiritual path and, more specifically, a vision quest. They believe that we are on Earth for a special reason, which is not always clear to us. This purpose is revealed through a sacred vision received on a journey into the wilderness. However, it is an arduous journey into the core of our being that should only be embarked upon with sincerity.

The quest is not only about receiving a vision; for the young Native American Indian, it is about facing fears, embracing the forces of nature and exploring his or her own identity in relationship to the world.

---

[8] http://www.native-americans-online.com/native-american-vision.html (accessed 29/10/2014)

So many of our problems are created by the insecurity that we are not accepted, do not have the resourcefulness to survive the realities of life on our own, or that we have nothing significant to offer the world. This fear is not necessarily based in reality. Walking alone into the wilderness is a very symbolic journey of facing up to the most fundamental fear of all humanity: abandonment. It is a critical Breakaway in which the young person will learn to fend for himself.

The Native Americans understand what adolescence does to young people. The degree to which their youth are guided through the process of embracing their independence will determine the success of their maturation. Nowadays there are a host of destructive vehicles that can be used to satisfy the growing need to experiment, impress our peers and rebel against authority.

These dangers breed fear in parents, who can become even more dominating, defensive and restrictive. This in turn leads to greater rebellion and a vicious cycle in which the young person comes to see destructive behaviour as part of their identity; instead of viewing healthy rebellion as a natural part of a transformation in the way they see themselves. If there's ever a time when young people need to understand and appreciate the dynamics of life, their individual purpose and community responsibility, it is during adolescence.

But this thing we call adolescence is not just limited to teenagers. People who have studied what we now call the mid-life crisis – another often radical identity overhaul suffered by people in the middle stages of their life – liken this phenomenon to a second adolescence.[9]

---

[9]   https://www.inkling.com/read/human-development-diane-papalia-ruth-feldman-12th/chapter-16/the-self-at-midlife-issues-and (accessed 3/10/2014)

A mid-life crisis involves more than just purchasing a flashy sports car. This second adolescence has resulted in affairs, divorce, the sabotaging of careers and even suicide. As a result, older people often also need a rite of passage in which they can Breakaway from their current ways of being in order to overcome the fears and pressures they are experiencing. It is possible for this phase to be a healthy stage of self-renewal involving greater creativity and a questioning of one's values.

Preparing for a quest

Critical to the vision questing process is the medicine man, who will prepare the adolescent for his passage into the spirit world. Knowing full well that the quality of the intention ahead of the experience will determine the quality of the vision, the medicine man works to first cleanse the seeker. This often includes spending time in a traditional sweat lodge where the vision quester is purified of toxins, bad spirits or negative energies.

The medicine man is a completely neutral force during the preparation for the experience. With the understanding that a parent or partner feels fear for their child or spouse and that they could influence their beliefs, the medicine man helps to open up the seeker's mind in order to allow a more authentic set of values to emerge. With no one around to influence him in the wilderness, the boy takes the opportunity to connect with his most natural being.

This is followed by preparation for a fast, which holds both meaning and practical value. Fasting is symbolic and a reminder of our ability to rise above even our most primitive urges and fears through practiced discipline. Fasting during a vision quest also makes the body more alert, as all of one's energy is dedicated to the quest.

The tribe is aware that a person who does not conform to the conventional norms of society could face expulsion from the tribe. On the deepest level, this could equate to potential starvation, abandonment and even death. Giving the seeker the skills to survive on his own allows him to embrace his own purpose without fear of banishment if he is unable to subsume to the tribe's values. Embracing the independence of the individual also gives the tribe's leadership the best opportunity to establish a rapport, so that the highest spiritual principles of the tribe can ultimately be perpetuated.

A seeker will be required to conduct a vision quest naked. The reason for this lies in a deep understanding that man's biggest problem is a lack of self-acceptance. It is about presenting yourself before the Great Spirit, without facades and defences, like the day you were born.

The virtue of solitude

The seeker heads up the highest mountain in the area alone, often at the mercy of dangerous animals, such as bears. Every encounter with nature, no matter how scary, is treated as a sacred gift and an opportunity to build faith in the universe. Although the preparation takes months, the seeker will only spend two to seven days on top of the mountain.

There, the seeker will create a sacred space with a fire in its centre. Thanks to his preparation with the medicine man, the young quester responds without emotion and consciously allows primal fears to run through his being. His senses are heightened as he receives guidance from the spirit world. With a deep awareness, the journey reveals natural laws that govern the interconnectedness of life and the need for adaptation, balance and sustainability. The seeker appreciates that his life has meaning in the dynamic web of life and understands those things that give his life the greatest purpose.

When the boy descends the mountain, he will sit with the medicine man, who will then help him to process the experience. What was learned? What visions were received? How does the initiate feel about his place in the world? After receiving a blessing from the medicine man, the seeker will be acknowledged by the tribe as an adult and begin to act on the vision that was acquired in the wilderness, which he and, most importantly, the rest of the tribe, regard as sacred.

The vision quest is the most important rite of passage for Native American Indian people. Although traditionally reserved for Native American men, women, too, quest in various forms all over the world. For centuries, various cultures have practised similar rituals or pilgrimages to prepare one for life's challenges. On the most famous pilgrimages of the Christian faith, The Way of St James, or El Camino de Santiago Compostela, draws thousands of people each year to walk a route along the Pyrenees Mountains, usually for 30 days. Buddhists make the long pilgrimage to Lumbini, Buddha's birthplace in the Himalayan Mountains of Nepal.

Most gap years fall far short of the effectiveness of the vision quest and other pilgrimages when it comes to setting, preparation, mentorship, unbiased support and quality reflection. As a result, many people return home with no better understanding of who they are than before they left home.

My gap-year experience also led me to believe that many Breakaways are falling short by not affording people the opportunity to complete a career imperative.

Before deciding what to study, I had a total of just one week's work experience – in an advertising agency. I decided on economics and business studies because of my intention to work in financial services, even though I had never spent any time in a financial institution. I have discovered while doing vocational coaching and speaking at different schools that this is the norm among many young people.

Around every passion is an industry

At the time of my gap year, I had no clear understanding of how many careers there were out there. I had no idea what else interested me, other than my passions for music and surfing – neither of which my father had encouraged as potential career choices. He, himself, had very little idea of the true range of the career landscape that could be explored on my own vision quest.

I assume that like most people, my father's ability to think laterally around careers was very limited. He had worked in one career for most of his adult life. When you mention music, such people tend to think "professional artist". When you talk of surfers, they think "competitive professionals", envisioning only the few people who have made it out of literally thousands who have tried. According to their beliefs, the rest who follow that road are struggling musicians or bum surfers with dreadlocks.

What my father could not see at the time is that around every passion, there is an industry, and around every industry, there are literally hundreds of careers. There are not just the people who make it and those who simply eke out a living: there is a whole spectrum of incomes.

People are no longer just working in the defined professional boxes that our parents once knew. Instead, there are people involved in a cluster of different careers that support their financial needs and their sense of purpose. Nowadays, opportunities for both specialisation and diversity are immense.

I could have spent my gap year designing surf trips around the world for people; working as an assistant to a top DJ; or as a crew member aboard the Sea Shepherd to help stop the poaching of whales and dolphins by the Japanese. There were literally hundreds of careers that would have had me jumping with excitement at the opportunity to learn. Instead, I was sent overseas to fulfill a career which, to the best of conventional wisdom and theoretical assumption, was the safest choice. Ultimately I turned to drugs.

Seeking pleasure

Two of the most significant challenges facing young people are career development and substance abuse. Most people don't fully understand the link between the two. At its most basic level, the brain is designed to direct the body away from pain and towards pleasure. Drugs and alcohol provide the most effective vehicles for allowing people to manipulate their state of mind and to avoid difficult emotions. Irrespective of how damaging a substance may be, it affords the user the power to instantly change how they feel.

A vocation encompasses all of the wholesome pleasures that make up a fulfilled life. It gives us the opportunity to express our deepest passions and allows us to make a contribution through our capabilities, while speaking to our highest values.

I knew that I loved the ocean the moment I felt its embrace all over my body. That is pleasure based on real experience. However, people often base their career decisions on theory, or an assumed pleasure. Most school and university curriculums are based on absorbing significant amounts of theory that are meant to lead us to careers that we will enjoy. We are told that if we follow conventional wisdom and subscribe to certain definitions of success, we will be fulfilled. That is the theory. However these theories no longer appear to be correct.

Unemployment, debt, depression and substance abuse are all signs that we are not adequately prepared for the wilderness.

Parents and schools cannot keep up with the pace of change, so cannot capture all of the available, meaningful opportunities in a structured way. Unable to make effective decisions of their own, adolescents become more susceptible to their parent's ideas about suitable careers.

The reality is that drugs and alcohol will always be a vehicle used by young people to escape confusion about their future, to medicate their feelings when their passions are squashed, and to rebel against the very tribe that raised them. Without any rite of passage to help them appreciate the nature of this journey, the young person is often not able to grow into a mature adult.

Make passion a viable alternative

Those little interests, desires and passions are the keys to our personal vision and mission. If someone lacks an empowering vision that is inspiring enough to provide an alternative to the pleasure gained from drugs, how can we expect that young person to say "No"?

The Rat Park study into drug addiction was conducted in the late 1970s by Canadian psychologist Bruce K. Alexander and his colleagues at Simon Fraser University in British Columbia, Canada. The researchers aimed to prove that addiction was less about the addictive substances themselves and more about the living conditions that would give rise to abuse.

They placed several heroin-addicted rats into two cages where they were able to drink water or continue to dose themselves with heroin-laced water. The only difference was in the cages: one was small, cramped and deprived of any device that would give the rats pleasure in the form of play. The other had all manner of wheels, balls and toys.

The rats that were able to play, chose only water, and eventually weaned themselves off the addictive heroin. However, the test cases that remained in the joyless cage continued to use the drug.

If parents would take a risk and embrace young people as responsible, independent and able to create their own reality, and just trust them enough to find the things that bring them joy, it would facilitate a conversation in which young people would realise how drugs and alcohol can take them away from their passions.

Quell the inner anger

This dynamic is not only limited to adolescents and addiction. The World Health Organisation estimates that by 2020, depression will become the world's most prevalent condition[10]. At least one in five people in the UK are said to be suffering from depression, and in the United States, the rate of antidepressant use has gone up 400% in two decades.[11] In South Africa, almost one in five people are said to suffer from mental illness.[12] Looking beyond the physiology of a chemical imbalance, depression is often spoken of as an internalised anger. Such anger stems from unmet expectations, the violation of values, the challenging of beliefs, and the threat to personal identity.

From a young age, parents instil in us expectations around what a successful life looks like. Our peers add an additional layer of the

---

[10] http://www.who.int/mediacentre/factsheets/fs369/en/ (accessed 4/10/2014)

[11] http://www.theguardian.com/society/2013/jun/19/anxiety-depression-office-national-statistics (accessed 4/10/2014)

[12] http://mg.co.za/article/2009-04-20-almost-one-in-five-south-africans-suffer-mental-illness (accessed 4/10/2014)

expectations that we need to meet in order to gain their acceptance. Then, on top of it all, marketers and advertisers prey on our deepest emotional needs, making us believe that buying a certain product will evoke a desired emotion within us.

The horrific statistics around depression and drug abuse suggest that we are riddled with unmet expectations. A vision of a successful life constantly drives us to up our expectations. Either we don't achieve an original notion of success, or we arrive at success feeling no different, realising that we have sacrificed our own values along the way. This is the source of many people's anger.

Depression also represents a fundamental inability to accept the nature of one's life and to process the emotions from the experiences that shaped it. M Scott Peck began his seminal book, *The Road Less Travelled*[13] with these words:

> *"Life is difficult. This is the great truth, one of the greatest truths. It is a great truth because once we truly see this truth, we transcend it. Once we truly understand and accept it, then life is no longer difficult."*

When the young Native American Indian seeker walks naked into the wilderness to give himself fully to his creator, he strips away all expectations for his life. He acknowledges that the wilderness of life is an unpredictable, challenging but ultimately real journey from which there is no escape. Bare as the day he was born, he acknowledges that he will leave this world with nothing but the knowledge that he embraced authentic values, natural laws and that he lived by conscious

---

[13]   *The Road Less Travelled*, M Scott Peck, Arrow;1978

principles. In the same way, we head off into the wilderness of career development to discover our spiritual vocation with an open heart and a curiosity that transcends expectation.

Your turn – Exploring potential interests

A key focus of the Breakaway is exposing yourself to things that sit beyond your horizon of experience: things that give your trip a sense of adventure, surprise and diversity. These can also become sustainable vocations.

You might consider bungee jumping a novelty that you have always wanted to try, but have never considered it as a potential career path. Completing this exercise will not only allow you to identify exciting things to explore on your Breakaway, it will help you to view each experience with a vocational filter so that you can take advantage of opportunities as they arise.

There is always a danger of getting lost in this process, so it is important that you keep up the momentum of the Breakaway design. Give yourself half a day to complete these answers, knowing that as you go along, you can always add ideas, places and careers to the framework that will be introduced in the next few chapters.

Draw on as many sources of ideas and inspiration as possible: magazines, websites, travel guides, blogs, Facebook etc.

⊕ ACTION

Please answer the following questions and save them in a journal or on a Word document on your computer:

1. What activities have you always wanted to try?
2. What careers have always interested you?
3. What products or brands impress you? What is it about these brands that appeals to your values?
4. Where have you always wanted to go?
5. Who inspires you, and why?
6. Write down the experiences that your friends have enjoyed that appeal to you. If necessary, ask them again for more details.

CALLING

Awaiting my welcome committee in the remote town of Puerto Montt, Chile, I could not have felt less welcome. Cut off by a slatted wooden screen, I waited in an entrance hall that had been furnished as if comfort was a sin. I sat on a stark wooden chair, staring at walls that had been left empty for fear of exciting the imagination and distracting this community from their primary function. One could be forgiven for thinking it was a prison, but these "inmates" were there of their own accord. They had voluntarily placed themselves in lifelong imprisonment in order to serve the Catholic faith. I was in the home of the Carmelite nuns and I was expecting the worst.

My visit to the nuns was accompanied by a full spectrum of emotions. Having grappled with organised religion all of my life, I found myself angry that somewhere along the line, the Vatican had convinced – or worse, manipulated – a group of woman to give up their families and children as well as the opportunity to enjoy a "full life experience" in order to serve God in complete isolation from the world.

The recollection of horror stories told by older generations who had grown up in convents only increased my apprehension that I was going to be greeted by a pack of abusive matriarchs wielding wooden spoons and crosses. I was sure that a life of such limited experience and opportunities for joy would eventually crush one's spirit, no matter how strong one's religious convictions were. For me, stories in the media of abuse by prominent Catholic figures had served as examples of exactly what happens when you deny human beings the most basic of needs. I could only imagine what happened inside this building when visitors were not around.

The door to the chamber opened. I felt like a juicy blood vessel, ready to have my life-force drained by vampires who would prey on my sins. I noticed first the white and brown clothes that exuded the creativity and energy of a funeral procession. Then, as I observed their faces, I braced myself for the grimaces of martyrs who had drained every ounce of pleasure out of their own lives as leverage to feed on my sinful indulgences.

But the women of various ages greeted me with smiles. They literally beamed with energy, vitality and enthusiasm. Their faces seemed to be as pure as the driven snow, and even though some of them must have been very old, they maintained a playful and caring demeanour.

Having started my career as a salesman, I would describe their welcome as flawless. Their first impression was perfect. These nuns were dealing with a disgruntled customer who was going to put their pitch to the test. But the pitch never came.

I soon realised that I was not sitting with a bunch of confused hell-raisers whose only salvation was a life of dogmatic isolation. Nor was I conversing with individuals with limited choices or life experiences. Among them were architects, engineers and teachers. These were real women who had experienced love, romance and international travel. Their parents had not persuaded them to sacrifice their lives to this calling. In fact, as I would discover, heartbroken loved ones had done all they could to prevent what they saw as voluntary incarceration.

So, why did they do it? They had lived normal lives, but they had chosen an extreme path. Society has gone to great lengths to escape the strict confines and dark history of the likes of the Inquisition in order to embrace individual autonomy, personal expression and freedom of choice. These ladies seemed to be going in the other direction: replacing freedom with isolation and substituting choice with dogma. But as I would learn, they felt that they had been chosen for this particular life.

The process of becoming a Carmelite nun is not easy. The sacrifices are unprecedented. As I learned, the journey to enrolling is different for each person. Yet they all spoke about experiencing the same thing – a Calling.

The word "vocation" has been used extensively in this book to describe the development of a meaningful career, but its roots are in religion, where those inspired by God, or perhaps those coerced into serving God, would dedicate their lives to their faith. One could be forgiven for suspecting that these women were the victims of some religious machine that had swallowed them at a young age and conditioned them into thinking in a certain way. The reality, however, was very different.

It takes seven years before a potential nun is invited to take the vow. There are no trapdoors set to swallow up people into religious servitude the minute they cross the threshold. Initially, these women can come and go from the convent as they please.

The power of a higher calling

I spoke to a 28-year-old nun named Carolina. She was one of the youngest women at the convent. She told me how when she had started her journey to becoming a Carmelite nun at the age of 21, she had had the opportunity to do a three-week stay, similar to the work experience offered by companies to graduates. These women are then sent back to the outside world to live their normal lives. This is to ensure that any choice they make is based on comparative reflection. The women can then decide whether or not to explore their calling further. Having completed a series of longer stays over a seven-year period, a new nun finally takes a vow and fully commits herself to the order of Carmelite.

So, what makes these women return to the point where they eventually give up their freedom altogether? The primary vocation of the Carmelite nun is to pray for us all. They isolate themselves from the outside world in order to remove any stimuli that could distract them from pure communion with the Holy Spirit. For these ladies, it is simple: the more they pray, the more they feel fulfilled. They do not stay in the convent out of a sense of duty. They are not bound by commitment or a fear of upsetting the order. They pray because it makes them feel better than they ever could while living in the outside world.

One nun even said that the nuns often see us, the people sitting on the other side of the screen, as the prisoners, stuck in a world of confusion in which we scramble around, trying to find wholeness through escapism, distractions and material possessions.

Sitting across from her, a wooden slat dividing us, I did indeed envy the clear sense of direction, energy and passion that this woman enjoyed in a setting that I would normally associate with rigidity and dogma. Where did my distrust of religion come from?

Spiral Dynamics, a book written by Don Beck and Chris Cowan[14], is a study of the development of human value systems. The authors believe that individuals within a society vacillate between the self and the community as the dominant value.

As infants, our dominant value of satisfying basic physiological needs reflects that of our early ancestor's primal survival mentality. To survive more effectively, we then have to sacrifice the normally dominant self in order to be accepted by a community that maintains safety and order through tribal traditions and customs.

As our early ancestors became more self-aware and able to question the meaning of life for the first time, they also became egocentric and started to challenge tribal beliefs. Once many of the myths and supernatural rituals that had maintained the tribal hierarchy had been tested and proved baseless, it was as if the very fabric of tribal community had to be unstitched and ripped apart during our society's adolescence. Individual egos, immature in the new freedom that came along with their ability to question their own meaning, became self-absorbed, greedy and exploitive. The world entered a period of chaos as the egocentric impulsiveness of our ancestors slowly destroyed the foundations of community.

Yet man still had to face his mortality and the fact that he did not know what came after death. Slowly, individual egos were quelled by leaders who wielded divine authority that was more powerful than man-made gods. They could send people to heaven or hell, depending on how well individuals fitted in to the divine plan that assigned people purpose, place and class. The principles of righteous living were

---

[14]   *Spiral Dynamics*, D. Beck and C. Cowan, Blackwell, 1996

enforced through constitutions; ranks; social classes; laws; and regulations.

The belief was that by sacrificing the impulses of the self, there would be a reward for obedience. Through subservience to the system, people found certainty, purpose and comfort in a chaotic world. However, in exchange for their salvation, they sacrificed their own meaning and individuality in exchange for absolutism.

The extreme attitude of this age was embodied by the Inquisition. Thousands of people were tortured and murdered for expressing their religious beliefs and individual meaning. People became so closed-minded over time that in the 16th century, they even threatened to put Galileo, a pioneer astronomer, to death for suggesting that Earth revolved around the sun and that our planet was not the centre of the universe. To prove what was ultimately a spiritual inspiration in the face of absolute dogma, Galileo and many other intellectuals had to develop what became the new religion in the age of enlightment: science

When I look back on my life, I definitely see a set of "coincidences" that have guided me to where I am now. I have no explanation for how I began to find some things highly enjoyable and others boring. Could genetics and my upbringing explain how I developed certain capabilities and innate talents? I don't like to admit that I am not in control of my own destiny, yet I do believe that there is a grand design in which I will express some form of vocation that is unique to me. Like Galileo who received inspiration after looking up to the heavens, I was also to receive a gift that I could not explain.

Yet interestingly, people brought up in the age of science often struggle with the idea that their career could, perhaps, have a spiritual dimension of its own. Ask most people if they pictured themselves in their current career and you will likely hear stories that reflect a limited ability to control or predict their destinies. Ask famous entrepreneurs where they got their best ideas and often they have no idea. When we embrace this spiritual axiom we realise that our decisions are guided equally by our intuition and inspiration as much as by a cognitive intellectualisation of where we can add value. For the nuns, it was the same.

* * *

At the end of my time at university, a career in the financial sector felt far from a calling. The rebellious nature of my adolescence meant that the divine authorities – my parents – saw me as a radical proposition whose egotistic expressions could not be trusted. Like the quelling of humanity's adolescence through religious indoctrination, my aspirations needed to be guided into a conventional career that guaranteed order, structure and success.

Little did I know that I was being channelled through the conventional grooves of society into pursuing the new basis for acceptance and salvation: money.

Galileo's inspiration would have greater consequences than just confirming our place in the solar system. His journey mirrored humanity's swing back to the dominant value of the self and the search for individual meaning. However, instead of raw and primal egocentricity, the self would be served by being strategic and entrepreneurial within a moral and legal framework. The emphasis shifted to individual achievement using science, materialism and Earth's "abundant" resources. We were gods once again as we sought to conquer the physical universe.

* * *

Cliffy was a modern-day embodiment of Zeus. He dominated the trading floor like a god shrouded in lightning bolts. As he hovered over his trading terminal, screaming orders that moved literally millions around the global markets, I was in awe of his power.

I was doing my internship at Merrill Lynch in Johannesburg, which I had managed to secure through nepotism. The team on the training floor did their best to keep me busy over the six weeks. Typically, they gave me the responsibilities at which even the most abused dog's body would turn up their nose. "We're testing to see if you have got what it takes to make it in this business!" was the usual excuse of those who handed over the worst jobs to keep me occupied.

The Morning Brief was a summary of the day's financial news that was circulated to all of the traders. I had to wake up at 4am and get to work in time for the newspaper deliveries so that I could summarise, in parrot fashion, all business news from the three main dailies. Once this had been delivered to Cliffy's email inbox by 6am, my day was pretty much free – except for a few important responsibilities, like running across the road to fetch lunch for the traders.

Boredom overcame me and I invented a way to sleep at my desk without getting caught. I would push one of the financial papers as close to my chest as possible so that I would actually have to put my head down almost 90 degrees to read the words on the page. The strategic placement of my reading finger at the bottom of the newspaper gave people the impression that I was religiously studying the latest news. I often slept for hours in this position. I am not sure whether the success of my technique could be attributed to how well I pulled it off, or my invisibility in the greater scheme of things. Eventually I was caught and sent home by Cliffy with a crash of thunder and a bolt of lightning.

I doubt they could have looked after me better at Merrill Lynch. They genuinely wanted to help me but there were bigger fish to fry. Even though I had done a three-year economics degree, there was a limit to what I could do at the company, given the high stakes of their game. Mine was an unstructured internship and despite attempts to create real objectives for me, I was just not engaged in the work. I am sure that the bank's proper graduate internship program geared for people who are inspired by the work must be an awesome experience and highly organised.

Even though I gained very little actual experience during my time at Merrill Lynch, I knew that I didn't want to be a banker the moment I saw Cliffy's eyes as I entered the office one morning at 5am. The sunken black sockets spoke of a complete lack of vitality and of many hours of sacrifice. He had already been in the office for half an hour and was awaiting the opening of the stock markets in Asia. He consistently worked 16-hour days, and I questioned, as I had with my father, why he was doing it. Even though I did not know Cliffy well, or what drove him, it seemed to me that his life was extreme.

Like early society's religious indoctrination was taken to the extreme, so too did mankind take his new-found individuality to the limits. Driven by the need to feel unique and significant, we competed to prosper in a world that had been ordered through status, celebrity and affluence. Driven to succeed at any cost, we would sacrifice our health, families, communities and even our planet in order to achieve our goals.

This extreme of societal development would lead to the whole new level of consciousness that society is experiencing now. There is a growing realisation that we cannot work unrelentingly without suffering consequences to our physical body and our family units. We cannot be focused on profit without protecting workers' rights, the environment and our corporate social responsibility, and we cannot exploit natural resources without upsetting the climate. When we got to the top and saw the trail of our destruction in our wake, it did not bring the sense of fulfilment that we sought.

Despite my lack of inspiration and limited work experience, I still pursued a career in finance. I was a year away from graduating with a masters degree in economics and business studies and I was financially and emotionally invested in following through with a career that would give my life some sense of order.

The nature of school is that people are told why things are important and what values they need to embody. This fundamental repression of personal passions, simply in the name of following through on societal values is exactly why many young people continue moving in directions that they do not enjoy. They have lost the ability to take responsibility for their own passions, or they have lost touch with their passions all together.

For years, I had been conditioning myself to follow a career that provided very few opportunities for me to express my passions and abilities, but still appealed to my dominant value: my ego. Being in finance meant making money; being powerful; having status; not only gaining acceptance from but also beating my peers in the rat race; and ultimately satisfying my father, a god of the Johannesburg legal fraternity.

The year after I finished university, my problems with addiction and alcoholism spiralled out of control. The truth was that I was completely lost. The only things that gave me pleasure in my life were substances. Unfortunately, they had become the basis of my identity and a coping mechanism to deal with my confusion and lack of higher purpose. The pleasure that I had experienced during early experimentation had been replaced with the need for a mindless escape from my feelings.

I was fortunate to discover Alcoholics and Narcotics Anonymous, two fellowships of people who share a willingness to give up drinking and drugs, respectively. Sitting in their meeting rooms at the age of 23,

I met people of all ages, walks of life and ethnic backgrounds. I was in the company of business owners, professionals and students. These were not people who lacked willpower or moral conviction.

As it turned out, alcoholism and drug addiction were for me and all of the other people in the meetings, just a symptom of a more serious spiritual bankruptcy from which we were all suffering.

Unable to fully explore my own sense of meaning or to trust my own expressions of self, my parents dogmatically influenced me to follow the path that represented order, success and acceptance, but which ultimately cut me off from the things that brought me fulfilment.

Only by hitting rock bottom did I realise that I was not God and that my selfish pursuit of ego had warped my instincts, relationships and ambitions. It was only then that I opened myself up to a new way of living – a spiritual way.

In fact, the only way I could stay sober was to build a relationship with a power greater than myself. This power could have been anything that gave my life meaning and that promoted the spiritual principles that ultimately provided a fulfilled life.

Like an onion, I stripped away all of the masks, fears, pressures and illusions that had been driving my destructive behaviour for so long. In many ways, it was the most significant Breakaway I have ever completed. I was able to let go of so much fear that had seen me bludgeoning my way to some idea of success that ultimately left me lost and without any sense of joy or acceptance of who I really was.

My experience of finding sobriety by building a relationship with a higher power had convinced me that there were indeed universal laws that dictated how we build relationship with everything around us. My egocentric attitudes about work were not going to be enough. My career had to extend beyond money and fear-induced control or acceptance. I had to figure out what I found meaningful, and then channel that into making a difference in people's lives.

* * *

I deeply respected the Carmelite nuns because they had consciously and incrementally explored their vocation. They had enjoyed the freedom to live a full life, to enjoy various professions and to explore the world before receiving their calling and making the sacrifices necessary for them to be of service. They had not been coerced, nor had they made decisions based on a fear of upsetting some established order. They had discovered what gave their lives meaning and they had followed that.

I made the decision not to go into a career in finance because I felt that I wanted to explore something more meaningful to myself. The problem was that I had completely lost touch with my passions and with other ideas about what I could do for a living. Like the Carmelite nuns, I would have to venture out again and discover my calling.

Your turn – Exploring your capabilities

Exploring and developing our capabilities is an incremental process. Like the Carmelite nuns, we have to be patient and conscious as we test our skills in the areas that fulfill our sense of calling. Over time we will understand where we add the most value and to enjoy the fruits that come from mastering a specific skill.

At the same time, we live in a world where we like to label things and to put them in boxes. How we can take a human being in all its infinite potential, and limit its value to a couple of lines on a CV? The whole essence of a Breakaway is about stepping outside of the box yet many people get frustrated that they cannot escape the well cut grooves of their existing skills and experience when they try to add value elsewhere.

This exercise is designed to clarify unique capabilities while doing a thorough inventory of your skills and experience. If this feels like filling in another job application, don't worry, the next chapter will literally shatter your perceptions of where you can add value.

⊕ ACTION

Please answer the following questions and save them in a journal or on a Word document on your computer:

1. Write down all your jobs of the past.
2. What value would you like to add to other people's lives?
3. If you would consider your vocation as achieving some kind of mission, what objectives would it include?
4. What would you say are your strongest capabilities that sit outside of your current job?
5. Do you have any capabilities that you have never considered? Also consider asking your parents, peers and colleagues.
6. What things do you do that you take for granted? Think of things that you do that are second nature to you.
7. If you have completed any career diagnostics or personality tests, what kind of capabilities do they propose to you as having that you have not previously explored?

6

THE BLANK CANVAS

KAROO DESERT

Making our way through the unforgiving desert, waves of heat emanated from the road, creating the impression that we were driving on a sizzling griddle pan. Bumping along one of the longest dirt tracks in Africa, our progress was slow. We knew that if we were not careful we would join the many before us who had suffered blow-outs while traversing this rugged path.

But had we experienced such misfortune we would not have remained stranded for long. Each year literally thousands of people drive this road out into the middle of nowhere to take part in a fascinating experiment in creative community-building in the heart of South Africa's Karoo Desert.

When pulling up to the entrance for the first time, it is customary to ring a large gong as a symbolic gesture of changing to a higher resonance – one of passion and creativity. As we stepped out of our warm vehicle, my friends and I were hit by the freezing desert night that bit at our fingertips like toothy rodents. But taking hold of the giant club, I hit the gong with all my might, sending my ethereal call up to the heavens. I had arrived at AfrikaBurn!

As we drew nearer the unfolding scene became increasingly bizarre. We may as well have docked on a brightly-lit mothership suspended in space. Unlike the grid lines of a typical city, this unique event space is designed in a massive archetypal circle that invites participation and unity by drawing people into the centre.

As we drove around the perimeter of the circle to look for our campsite, strange vehicles began to emerge from the darkness, like eerie sea creatures. An old sailing ship on wheels floated past, revellers partying on its deck, while a classic Mini Cooper covered in grass, and a vintage bus, did their rounds. Once at the event, no cars are allowed, unless they have been transformed to such a degree that they are approved by the DMV – Department of Mutant Vehicles. We found our spot and joined the group with which we would be collaborating – Camp Partycipation.

The following morning we awoke to discover that the AfrikaBurn space in which to unleash one's imagination came in the form of a dry, desolate, lunar landscape. It felt like a different planet and the festival itself seemed other-worldly. The blank desert canvas had been transformed into a melting pot of creative expression. Amazing sculptures – some 50ft tall – dotted the landscape, and creativity camps led people through a host of experiences designed to open the mind and the heart.

"Burners", no matter how famous and successful, had left what defined them back at home. Their professions, social standing, race and education were no longer of any consequence. Instead, they embraced a fantastical and meaningful expression of themselves. The energy of 5 000 people breaking through all of their inhibitions took my breath away.

Staring out over the chaos, I felt something stir inside of me. It was as if the desert canvas that was bursting to life was inviting me to splash the picture with my own colour. I danced in ways that I had never before moved my body, and I began to talk to complete strangers, with no expectations other than curiosity of what might emerge. I embraced the whole event with an open heart – no agenda, just fascination.

AfrikaBurn is an offshoot of the Burning Man Creative Arts Festival, which started with the burning of a 20ft sculpture of a man by a handful of people on a beach at dusk in San Francisco, 1986. This act of artistic expression happened for no other reason than it seemed like a fun idea at the time.

By 2010, the "man" had grown to a staggering 75ft tall, and its burning had become the symbol of a gathering that became known as Black Rock City – a completely man-made community in the Nevada Desert. The six-day event is attended by 50 000 people from all over the world. In 2010, then in its fourth year, AfrikaBurn was attended by approximately 5 000 people. In 2014, about 10 000 people attended the event. "Burns" are now held all over the world.

The event's energy and culture stem from the practise of its key principles. The first is the gift economy. Nothing is for sale at a Burn. Participants are required to bring along what they need in order to survive in the desert. More importantly, they are invited to offer a gift, which could be anything from the erection of a massive art installation to simply offering people wet wipes as they come out of a toilet.

All that the organisers do is provide the canvas. Everything that happens at the festival is prompted by the participants. The community takes ownership of the event as a whole. At AfrikaBurn, the feeling of unity is as strong as the hard earth that holds the space in which the community creates.

It is no coincidence that some of the world's leading innovators, such as Sergey Brin of Google, and Elon Musk of SpaceX, attend Burning Man events. To the ignorant, they are viewed as hedonistic parties that take place in the middle of deserts, but for those who understand their true essence, they are platforms for creativity like no other.

There, in the middle of the Karoo, I discovered for the first time people who were not creating for the sake of financial return – they were creating for the fulfilment of seeing something that had been burning in their imaginations finally being birthed. When people engaged with one another, it was on the purest and most accepting level, as they embraced each others' creative expression. With no rules or framework of what was acceptable, the diversity and creativity in what people produced was quite extraordinary.

Embrace innovation

The essence of a Breakaway is to discover ways in which to explore that which we find meaningful, and then to translate that into a vocation that will add value to our lives and those of others. We all have a unique set of passions, values and abilities that, when understood and appreciated, can help to create a far richer life experience.

The challenge, however, is to be innovative. We can develop as many products and services as we like, but if they do not add value to people's lives they will generally not amount to a sustainable vocation. The definition of innovation, therefore, is a unique product or service that meets people's needs in new and more effective ways. But innovation should not be limited to those people who want to start their own businesses. More than ever, companies require their employees to solve problems using creative solutions.

For something to be new and unique it has to sit outside of the normal confines of thinking – it has to be out of the box! As a result, you cannot have innovation without creativity. Across every industry, it is the people who pushed boundaries who have created the more innovative and desirable products. These are not always radical innovations, such as the mobile phone or the digital camera. Often the most valuable innovations are incremental improvements on existing products. Think of the iPod. This legendary product, first released in 2001, was seen as radical innovation, but it was actually an incremental improvement on existing technology. The first MP3 player, Diamond Multimedia's Rio PMP300 player, became widely available in the United States in 1998.

If you cannot have innovation without creativity, then you definitely cannot have creativity without passion. Passion provides the fuel that spurs us to continue pushing boundaries. Passion provides the opportunity to experience sheer inspiration as well as the freedom to be ourselves – to create and express our craziest notions without inhibitions. Passion comes from within us. It cannot be explained or denied.

Considering the importance of creativity to both personal fulfilment and success, it is quite extraordinary how little of our formal education is dedicated to creativity and to creative problem-solving. If anything, we are educated away from creativity and into narrow, predetermined ways of thinking.

Most of us attended schools that have a bias towards specific subjects. We were invited to join societies rather than be allowed to invent our own. They even made us wear the same uniforms. Youths who are driven by peer pressure can be ruthless. Anything that sits outside of the parameters of "cool" is crushed, along with the acceptance of any radical form of self-expression.

While experimenting with new careers, my challenge was to discover a place in which I could truly be groundbreaking while exploring the depths of my creativity, uninhibited by any rules, boundaries or pressures that would encourage me to conform to the status quo.

In the workplace we are trained to think within specific mindsets. At home we are expected to live in a certain way and we are influenced by the social beliefs that our communities deem acceptable. Little did I know that I would find one of the most amazing spaces for discovering not only my creativity, but also new potential vocations, in one of the harshest environments on Earth.

My presence at AfrikaBurn was no mistake. Having got sober the year before and been through a recovery process in which I took responsibility for my own fulfilment without the need for substances, I also took responsibility for my own values and passions. Instead of returning to the United Kingdom, I moved to Cape Town, where I could be close to the ocean.

Instead of buying into the fear that South Africa was degenerating into mayhem, I committed to being a part of what had become a miraculous transformation. I started DJing and I bought a surfboard. But, even though I had committed to my values, I still had no idea what I could do as another career.

One day, my girlfriend showed me an advert for a job at a company called Red Zebra. The company used music and creativity to facilitate both personal and organisational development. Even though it felt strangely different from the more corporate job advertisements that I had been reading, something inside told me to give it a go.

As I walked into the office, I immediately had a good feeling. A man named Mark got up to greet me. Unlike at the suit-dominated Merrill Lynch, Mark was dressed casually and his curly afro exuded the same wild creativity as his demeanour.

Mark would become instrumental in my life on multiple levels. Besides becoming an amazing friend and mentor, he would expose me to a side of career-building that I had never before known. Mark had grown up in both the United Kingdom and South Africa. The son of a

British woman and a Colombian musician whom he had never met, he had been adopted in England.

Mark had personified the image of the struggling musician. His daily routine had involved playing the djembe and didgeridoo on Brighton Pier, unaware of how he could use his passion for music to do anything else other than to perform. He used to hang around the various busking points until he had enough money to buy marijuana. He had been on the dole, the British welfare system. It was his only real source of income.

Mark would meet his partner and best friend, Oliver, at a "squat party". These events involved protesters barricading themselves in empty houses that were scheduled for demolition in order to make way for massive developments. The new buildings were going to destroy acres of lush English countryside, so the squatters felt that it was their duty to protect the Green Belt, a ring of green just outside of London. Mark holed up in the attics and lofts of these houses for months, sometimes bringing development to a complete halt.

Mark and his partner, Ollie, decided that they had to use their collective passion for music to make a difference – to add value to people's lives. They wanted to give everyone the gift of playing music. The question was: how?

The pair developed a very effective facilitation technique that would allow them to walk into a room of complete strangers, many of whom had never played an instrument before, and in under an hour turn them into a fully organised band that rocked out on amazing rhythms played on a variety of different instruments. The key to their technique was that they facilitated people making their own rhythms, rather than playing the role of conductors, who taught people to play established songs in parrot fashion.

They converted normal people from passive listeners of music into active catalysts in the creation of music. Using the metaphor of people coming together to learn how to play harmonious music, they applied it to many different issues in companies, schools and communities. Mark went from being a busker who eked out a living, to a world leader in facilitation. He has worked in more than 65 countries and has facilitated groups as large as 10 000.

It was fascinating to see how Mark lived his life and how he had been able to create a business that gave him an amazing lifestyle. When he wasn't playing in a local samba band, he was jetting off to facilitate a global event under the Pyramids at Giza.

I had always wanted a mentor, and if you had asked me five years before what kind of mentor I would have wanted, it would probably have taken the form of an archetypal power player – a captain of industry sitting in an ivory tower: intimidating, egotistical and driven by ways to create more money. But Mark was different. His humble office was located on Green Market Square, one of Cape Town's cultural hubs. It was filled with hundreds of instruments and African designs. There was always music blaring.

Mark opened my eyes to creativity, conscious values and to the idea of having a purpose beyond the pursuit of making money. He showed me that work could be a fun place, too. Compared to my friends who were working in London and Johannesburg, I was earning a pittance, but every single day I woke up looking forward to work. The money would come later, I said. And it did.

Search for your stars

As I escaped the chaos of the AfrikaBurn festival, which had served as the perfect metaphor for the tangent that I had gone on in my career, I sat out in the middle of the desert alone. Looking up into the most amazing sky I had ever seen in my life, the heavens in all their glory unfolded above me.

When the organisation that was creating the Square Kilometre Array – what would become the Earth's largest radio telescope – had to find the location with the clearest skies, they chose the Karoo in South Africa. You do not know the stars until you have been to this magical place. Literally billions of galaxies that I had never seen before presented themselves with crystal-clear clarity. Many of humanity's greatest stories come from man finding meaning by looking up into the sky. I was visiting the greatest theatre on Earth.

The completely narrow sense of career potential that I felt in my youth can be likened to the dull skies we enjoy in cities, oblivious to what lies beyond the haze of light and pollution.

Another reality is that the ideas that shape our lives do not develop in a linear fashion. If that were the case the night sky would be completely black, except for one line of uniform stars extending into space. Looking up into the heavens as we dream of a future, one is greeted by billions of interconnected stars, galaxies and black holes that are actually all feeding off each others' energy in a cosmic dance.

What is truly astounding is that if one compares the Hubble Space Telescope images with those of brain scans, they look exactly the same: A galaxy of neurons that represent the faculties of imagination, memory, emotions and sensory stimulation that all cross pollinate to create new, meaningful opportunities.

My experience with Red Zebra had shown me another star in my sky. Working with Mark was not going to turn me into a hippie squatting in a loft to prevent urban development, any more than attending AfrikaBurn was going to turn me into a nomad who rejected the financial system. However, it gave me an experience that would allow me to come to terms with all of the opportunities available to me in a constellation that included all of my passions, values and abilities.

Your turn – The Career Constellation

The fact that there are an immeasurable number of available careers out there might baffle you. Perhaps you can't think of more than 20 that could be viable options for you right now. Just remember, every occupation has subtle nuances, variations and styles that allow for diversity. With enough of a market, they can become sustainable careers.

If you struggle to see this, then perhaps you are still thinking along the conventional lines that have been ingrained in you since childhood. You'll need to be a blank canvas on which to paint a much bigger picture of your potential.

Career options are changing all of the time. As a new career develops, another one becomes redundant. A person who is fed up with commercial law could suddenly develop a whole new love for his career by practising law in areas that are more aligned to his passions and values. This might mean becoming a lawyer for a professional golfer or education campaigner, or even protecting the rights of an endangered animal. Attached to every traditional profession are many additional options that are being created every day through the cross-pollination of new ideas, industries and careers.

Creating your career constellation

Let's try a cross-pollination exercise. In its most basic form, let's attempt what innovators and entrepreneurs do when developing new products: think laterally.

⊕ ACTION

1. Open up a new spreadsheet on your computer. Create two columns. Type in **Career Constellation** as your heading.

2. Label the first column **Vocational options**. Looking over your answers in the previous chapters, evaluate everything you have written in order to create your own individual list under the heading. When deciding what goes on your list consider the following important differentiators and the example to follow:

   - If you get stuck trying to work out the difference between a **passion** and a **value**, ask yourself this question: Do I do this because I love it or because I feel it is important? Having a nice house might be important to you, yet you are clearly not passionate about the idea of property, interior design or landscaping. You may love your family and feel that spending time with them is important, yet you are clearly not passionate enough about it to explore family-related vocational options, like family therapy or designing family-focused holidays. If you are still stuck, write it down on your list anyway.

   - If you have an **interest** in something, but have yet to experience it on your Breakaway, write it down. Its purpose will become clear.

   - Professionals break down your previous jobs and specific skills into **mini professions**, irrespective of the passion and value you have for them.

   - Graduates, write down all of the **skills** that allow you to add value in the present moment. For example, a marketing student's ability to organise a survey.

   - Capabilities can often be very vague. For example, being good with people can have a number of potential vocations connected to it. At the same time, there are specific careers that are designed for people who are good at building relationships, such as sales, public relations and management. If you are not clear how your capabilities apply to different vocational options, ask your parents, friends or a career website. Be sure to quiz people who are knowledgeable in career development. Type the various **vocational options** connected to your broad **capabilities** in the first column, in separate rows.

• Consider all the places you want to visit on your Breakaway (for example, Brazil), as well as where you live now, as vocational options. You may be able to apply or explore vocational options in a specific place, or your vocation may be the place itself.

3. You should now have a very long list containing exciting potential, but also repetition. Look over your whole framework and delete any repetitive vocational options in Column 1.

4. Create a heading for the second column: **Expanded vocational options**.

5. If you have no experience in a vocational option that is related to a passion, such as music, research as many careers as you can related to each of your options and list what you discover as **Expanded vocational options** in Column 2. If you are not sure, go on to the internet and type in "careers + your particular passion". An example would be careers + music. You should be able to gain an overview all of the established vocational options. Then list them in Column 2.

6. **Important:** Do not do this if you have already broken down your old professions, experience, or skills from studying into mini professions. Just carry these over into Column 2: **Expanded vocational options**.

Example of a Career Constellation

I have tried to keep this theoretical example as simple as possible while demonstrating the key differentiations that you will need to make.

Vocational option	Expanded vocational options
Music – General passion of someone with no experience in a given industry.	DJ Producer Record label owner Sound engineer
Bungee jumping – Specific interest or experience desired on a Breakaway that could become a potential vocation.	Bungee jumping
Ledger balancing – Mini profession distilled out of the overall profession of accounting.	Ledger balancing
Partying – Key value that interests youth enough to engage in work experience.	Party planner Events organiser Club rep
Walking on the beach – general passion and daily activity that can become a vocational option.	Tour guide
Sewing – Key skill that a fashion graduate could use to add value to the market.	Sewing
Watching TV – Key daily activity that can engage people to explore a vocation.	Film critic TV producer Advertising
Dogs – passion.	Vet Dog minder
Rugby – passion.	Coach Commentator Player

Vocational option	Expanded vocational options
Vintage – specific style about which a person is passionate.	Vintage clothing designer, Vintage clothes retailer
German – language.	German
Good with people – Key capability that could be a vocational option.	Social media Public relations
Brazil – Country to be visited on a Breakaway where all manner of vocations can be explored or developed.	Brazil

This is where you get creative and truly explore all of the vocational options available to you. The objective here is to cross-pollinate your expanded vocational options to see what interesting ideas emerge. All you need to do is combine one vocational option with all of the other vocational options in the other rows.

 Examples: Music producer + dogs = ?

     DJ + bungee jumping = ?

Remember, the most important thing at this stage is that there is no such thing as a bad idea. Your objective is to come up with as many options as possible, even if some of them do not make sense.

 Combining the profession of being a music producer with a passion for dogs might allow someone to come up with an idea for producing music that relaxes dogs that bark too much. Is it a crazy notion or the next big thing? Who knows? Study the example below and then apply the principles to your list.

Vocational options	Expanded vocational options
Music	DJ Producer Record label owner Sound engineer Organising music events DJing at parties Creating playlists for parties Organising beach music events and festivals Creating beach-walking compilations Creating TV music playlists Music reality shows Creating music that relaxes dogs Creating rugby anthem compilations.
Bungee jumping	DJing at bungee jump sites Organising bungees at music events and beach festivals Creating music compilations for bungee sites Creating reality shows for bungee jumping Bungee jumping for dogs (Cruel, but it's an idea) Organising global bungee tours for enthusiasts.
Ledger accounting	Accounting for music bands; DJs or record labels; festivals; films and documentaries; rugby clubs; or any other organisation included in your passion.
Partying	Party planning Events organising Club repping Organising beach parties Leading parties on exotic beach-walking holidays Filming party events Organising dog events Organising events and hospitality for rugby games Organising socials and trips away for friends or to Brazil.

Vocational options	Expanded vocational options
Walking on the beach	Becoming a tour guide Producing travel shows based on walking the great beaches of the world Walking other people's dogs on the beach Organising beach rugby Organising social beach-walking trips.
Sewing	Sewing costumes for rock bands or DJs and for music videos Creating special outfits for people who want to bungee jump in superhero outfits, like Superman Creating costumes for events or festivals Creating walking clothes for the beach Creating costumes for TV or film Creating cute dog outfits Sewing rugby jerseys or supporter paraphernalia Creating outfits for friends.
TV programmes and film	Becoming a film critic TV producer Advertising Producing dog shows Producing rugby shows Filming friends' special events.
Playing with my dog	Vet Dog minder Dog rugby Organising dog-based social events with friends.
Rugby	Coaching Commentating Player Organising rugby trips overseas. Opening a social venue related purely to rugby.

Vocational options	Expanded vocational options
Vintage	Collecting vintage music Organising parties with vintage themes Sewing vintage clothes Collecting vintage rugby jerseys Collecting or showing vintage movies Organising social events where people exchange vintage clothes Going to Brazil to find vintage items that can be sold in my home country.
German	Collecting or producing German music Selling music to German people Working as an accountant in Germany Organising or attend parties in Germany Organising bungee jumps in Germany Walking the northern German beaches.
Socialising with my friends	Social media Public relations.
Brazil	Working as an actor in Brazil Playing rugby in Brazil Organising a trip to Brazil with friends Hosting Germans in Brazil.

I hope you are starting to see how this process can help you to identify an array of potential vocations. Obviously, the more extensive the list, the more choices you will have. So, if need be, go through the process one more time. Put as much time as you can into it. After all, you are identifying the options that will start a chain reaction that could influence the rest of your life.

EL DORADO

I was hugely disappointed in Machu Picchu. This ancient, secret Inca kingdom that has graced the covers of thousands of travel brochures has been lorded as the highlight of any trip to South America and had been on my hit list for a long time. However, after visiting the city, it took me a while to clarify what I wanted to write about the experience. For me, it was not a show-stopper.

Without a point of comparison, my first impressions were positive, and I continued on my trip thinking that I had ticked the mystical quest box. It was only when I discovered another lost city in the heart of Colombia that I realised Machu Picchu was not the Holy Grail.

We are all seeking our own El Dorado, a magical city of gold that, beyond fame and treasure, provides a journey of challenge and character-building. Nowadays travellers have to go further, faster and to more extreme lengths than ever before just to feel that they are breaking boundaries. This likely raises the expense, the risk to one's safety, and the opportunity for disappointment. The key, therefore, is to walk a fine line between throwing one's self into the complete unknown, where things are dangerous and uncharted, and slotting into the well-trodden grooves of popular, organised and well-reviewed experiences.

I believe the lost city of Ciudad Perdida is one such experience. The lost city is on the cusp of being discovered by the masses. Founded about 800 AD, some 650 years earlier than Machu Picchu, it is the royal city of the Tairona people and is located in what has become known as the Sierra Nevada National park in Columbia.

The tribe leaders lived in the city for centuries, but regular tribe members were only allowed to visit the holy place to perform important rituals. Besides an unquenchable thirst for gold, the invading Spanish conquistadors also brought a host of new diseases to the continent – one of which found its way into the Tairona community. When people started to get sick in the holy city, illness was interpreted as a bad omen and the whole sanctuary was abandoned for hundreds of years.

Ciudad Perdida was first discovered by the modern world in 1965, when tomb raiders uncovered the ancient graves of the Tairona leadership while searching for gold and other precious metals. The lost city only came to the attention of the authorities in 1975 because of infighting among the tomb raiders. The Colombian army has been protecting the city ever since then.

As a gateway to the Sierra Nevada, the city of Cartagena is one of the most beautiful colonial port towns I have ever seen. Walking through the cobbled streets one can almost hear the faint echoes of pirates and traders and cannons firing at invading ships, led by the likes of 16th century explorer Sir Francis Drake. This prized town was seized by countless competing empires and then lost again to yet another invader in a haze of gun powder.

It was a golden age of exploration in which the highest honour was to head off into the unknown to discover and conquer foreign lands and bring back new treasures, along with tales of adventure that enthralled the masses. As modern-day conquistadors with not much left to conquer, Emma and I would spend our time salsa dancing the night away, taking in the cool ocean breeze on the old port fortifications and imagining what it would be like to conquer new worlds.

One can catch a train and a bus to the top of Machu Picchu without even breaking a sweat, but to reach Ciudad Perdida, one has to drive for eight hours and then trek for five days through jungle that would put Indiana Jones through his paces. At the beginning of the adventure we had to cross an army checkpoint. The area is still a hot spot for conflicts with the Fuerzas Armadas Revolucionarias de Colombia (FARC) communist rebels. This only added to the excitement.

On our way to Machu Picchu we stayed in hostels that offered up clean sheets and fans to keep the heat at bay. Our trip to Ciudad Perdida found us sleeping outdoors in hammocks covered by mosquito nets, all the while knowing that lurking out in the darkness were all manner of creepy crawlies looking for a warm place to spend the night.

What makes Ciudad Perdida unique is that it is has no reason to expand or grow. Fortunately, the Colombian government recognised the need to protect native tribal culture and offered to subsidise any expenses that might cause the Tairona people to abandon their traditional way of life. This will hopefully ensure that Ciudad Perdida offers a true lost city experience for some time to come.

Fully content to continue as they have done for hundreds of years, the tribe have no need to exploit the lost city for monetary gain. As a result, they only allow 3 000 visitors into the city each year. Machu Picchu grants 2 500 permits each day.

At Machu Picchu it is difficult to feel that one is in the midst of a lost city as one gets caught in the stampede of tourists and camera flashes, and where one can buy a caramel latté and smoked salmon bagel at the coffee shop on top of the mountain.

By comparison, at Ciudad Perdida, taking photographs of the local tribe without their permission is strictly forbidden. In a community that has resisted dehumanising its inhabitants like animals in a zoo, we got to experience their tribal way of life as guests of a kingdom.

One day I came across a lone child sitting on a rock staring out into the distance. Dressed in a traditional, plain, cloth garment, muddied from years of childish exploration in the jungle, his face radiated purity. I wondered if he had ever been out of the jungle, and what he would make of what we call "civilisation".

The small child noticed my iPod. I was pretty confident that he had seen an MP3 player before but that he had never listened to any of the electronic music that I preferred, so I was fascinated to see his reaction.

As I placed the earphone in his ear and pressed play, I watched his eyes grow wide as the new beats resonated in his mind for the first time. I felt like a proper missionary, spreading the gospel of house music. Eventually, after prying my device from his hands, I could not help think that, as a human race, we will never be satisfied. We are all searching for something.

There I was, hungry to escape the noise, freneticism, technology and the mundane realities of life in the city, but still trying to rip my iPod – a symbol of the Western obsession with development – out of the hands of a young child, who represented the essence of the ancient kingdoms and way of life I was trying to rediscover.

The route to the lost city was very challenging and traversed massive hills as we ventured further into the heart of the Colombian jungle. This was made more difficult by the frequent heavy rains that transformed the paths into gauntlets of slippery mud.

Emma, obviously not descended from the great British explorers, decided to brave the route in the equivalent of squash shoes, which slowed us down significantly. We playfully threatened her that she would be offered as a sacrifice when we eventually arrived at the lost city. Still, we crossed dozens of rivers, which gave us ample opportunity to swim in crystal-clear pools and jump off cliffs into amazing water-falls.

On the third day we arrived at the foot of Ciudad Perdida. I finally understood how it could have been lost for a thousand years. To access the city we had to climb a very well-concealed flight of stairs that ascended vertically for what felt like hours. The path was still in perfect condition, untouched by human hands since the time the city was deserted.

Upon reaching the summit at midday, we were greeted by a com-pletely empty space that allowed our imaginations to run wild. The city consisted mainly of empty platforms on which we could envision all manner of ceremonies, sacrifices and offerings being made to the Tairona leadership, who perched high above their followers, bedecked in gold.

An early map of the area carved into rock depicted the intersections of the great rivers and mountain peaks – the vital landmarks that the people of the day would use to navigate huge tracts of jungle.

Summiting the high ground of the city, I could see nothing for miles around. It took me back to my time at Machu Picchu, which also had amazing vistas. However there, one could not avoid looking directly onto a hydroelectric plant that altogether dashed any feeling of mysticism.

Leaving Ciudad Perdida in the late afternoon there were further days of exhausting walking out of the jungle ahead of us – enough time to ponder a truly awesome experience. I felt that I had finally come closer to that feeling of discovering an ancient lost city for myself.

Despite my experience I still felt that urge to discover something untouched and unique. The Sierra Nevada tour was as authentic as it could be, but ultimately, it was packaged, well regarded and visited by 3 000 people a year. My soul was screaming out to explore unchartered terrain, rather than following well-trodden paths.

Finding the unmapped route

Travel will always be the main vehicle used by humanity to satiate that feeling of discovery, but unfortunately in the 21st century, there is very little on Earth that has not been mapped, reviewed and packaged. Every peak has been climbed, every pole reached, the globe circumnavigated and rivers mapped.

It has been a long time since we have read about a journey to a new land or the discovery of a new species or remote culture that has been lost in time. Space travel was the last frontier of exploration and with Nasa scaling back its budgets and focusing mainly on Mars, we may be denied tales of humans exploring other planets, just to see what is there.

The modern-day explorers in chief are the innovators who conquer new markets, realms of knowledge and art – pioneers who push the boundaries of exploration into new worlds. Just as venturing into unknown territories has its risks, discovering our own unique vocation requires courage. One has to face the risks of making a few wrong turns and dealing with unexpected obstacles while continuing on, when every part of you wants to return back to the safety of a conventional career.

Perhaps vocation development is the last epic journey available to us. We all have a completely unique set of passions, values and abilities. Like a fingerprint, no two vocations are alike, and our journey to discover this magical key to our lost city of fulfilment is perhaps the great quest of our age.

Just as adventures to discover lost cities are not for everyone, vocation development is a scale that varies in the level of entrepreneurship, innovation and outright craziness that people are prepared to embrace. Some people do not feel the need, nor have they the constitution, to go out and discover their own lost cities. They are happy to stay at home and enjoy the certainty and security that comes from sticking to a safe path. For others, dancing mechanically to the same well-grooved records is the antithesis of the spirit that burns inside of them.

* * *

Sitting at my desk at Red Zebra, there was something burning inside me. It had been bubbling below the surface for some time. Slowly, desire was taking over my whole being. Having watched Mark manifest his passion in a voyage of self-discovery, I felt that I too wanted to explore and create my own adventure by starting a business. It begged the questions: What was my vision? What gave me a sense of purpose? What was the ideal business that I wanted to discover?

I spent months doing indepth research, reflection and conceptualisation. No tool was spared as I plumbed the very depths of my being. Mind maps, lists and journals overflowed with potential. At the end of it, I decided that I wanted my business to focus on nature, personal development and travel.

During my recovery from addiction, I had spent a significant amount of time in nature. I found that being immersed in the wilderness provided me with a sense of having a unique place in this world.

Nature offers up a myriad of different organisms that do what comes naturally to them in an interconnected system that is as beautiful as it is miraculous. I was inspired to use the great outdoors as a vehicle to connect people to that sense of purpose, and to use it as a guide for personal and business growth. Adaptation, balance, sustainability and integrity. Nature has so much to teach us. I love being outside and the idea that it would become my office was hugely exciting.

During my recovery and time at Red Zebra, I had been inspired by the art and science of personal development. Various tools and resources had made a significant difference to the quality of my life and I wanted to share them with people who were also struggling to find their way. Personal development work was being conducted in corporate boardrooms, stuffy hotel conference halls and claustrophobic counselling chambers. I thought the great outdoors would be the ultimate venue for this type of work and a key innovation.

Finally, I had a desire to travel. I asked myself what I would like to have achieved by the time I was on my deathbed, and I came to realise that I would like to feel I have seen the greatest miracles of nature – the Himalayas, the Grand Canyon and the Arctic.

The result was a business called Elixir. Its core business function was to offer nature-based personal development experiences in some of the most beautiful places on Earth. The Elixir, from Paulo Coelho's famous book, *The Alchemist*, was used to turn base metals into gold. This was a perfect analogy for the experiences I wanted to create for my clients. Through the business, I was able to visit some of the most amazing wilderness areas in South Africa, along with the Himalayas and the Scottish Highlands.

So I continued on my epic voyage to discover my El Dorado, my ultimate vocation. Like all treasure hunters seeking the Holy Grail, I eventually realised that the prize was not made of gold or silver, but could be found in the blood, sweat and tears of making the journey. The real treasure came in the form of powerful lessons, new friends, amazing memories and a richer perspective on the world.

Your turn – The Vocational Dashboard

Exploration is a divergent process – it expands outwards, often exponentially. Your dreams, desires, interests, goals and ideals all start to paint a picture of the sky that radiates with thousands of connected opportunities.

Even though you have the opportunity to paint a better picture of who you are as an individual and of the world around you, you will still need to pin down the first few steps of your plan. The nature of creative problem-solving is that after diverging, you need to converge on your biggest priorities in order to focus your time, money and energy on your Breakaway.

People who seek their own El Dorado have to face huge challenges. Besides leaving the safety of traditional careers, they have to overcome significant obstacles as they try to manifest their unique vision. You cannot overcome these challenges without passion. This is the fuel that will keep you going when you are lost in the jungle of your destiny.

Exploration brings more choice and complexity

When you explore, you are giving yourself more options, but this brings greater complexity. The reality is that we live in the 21st century, and we are constantly exposed to people's new adventures, emerging innovations, and changing perspectives on life. The only way to detach ourselves from this growing buffet of choices would be to cut ourselves off from all communication and media, which would be impossible for most of us.

The amount of available information is increasing daily. Every day we have to contend with Twitter, Facebook, LinkedIn, Meet Up and a host of other mediums that blast us with opportunities. Just opening ourselves up to exploration can be overwhelming, confusing and distracting. We could even be bumped off our vocational path. When it becomes difficult to choose, it often feels easier not to make any choice at all – or even worse, to let someone choose for us.

Setting a powerful intention

Another reason to make choices is that there is something powerful about setting an intention. With a strong desire, motive, emotional objective or ideal, we can literally change our realities. A Breakaway takes commitment, courage and hard work. At times you will feel financial insecurity or emotional uncertainty. Committing your intention to a Breakaway allows you to face your fears head-on so that you can make big decisions from the right place.

Jack-of-all-trades, Master of none

You may come across many opportunities that you want to leverage. However, you have to be open to the vocational power that comes from specialisation and from being able to focus money, time and energy.

Your career can be based around a host of clustered activities that support your sense of purpose and financial requirements, but this approach must be a conscious process, rather than simply the outcome of throwing yourself into hundreds of activities without gaining traction.

Clarifying your best vocational options

For those of you who are in the early stages of your vocational development and using a Breakaway as a vehicle to experiment with vocational options for the first time, you may be uncertain of your true level of passion or ability. There is no substitute for experience. Having evaluated your options in the previous chapter, you will now need to make decisions about where to first get real experience. You'll need to trust your intuition when doing so.

Preparing to clarify your best vocational options

Look at your **Career Constellation**, which contains all of your **Expanded Vocational Options**. As part of this convergence process, we will create the first few filters that will help you to evaluate the vocational options you have discovered. These filters will also assist you to manage your opportunities and allow your most passionate ones to emerge.

Filter 1 – Intuitive excitement

This key ranking is out of five stars. It allows you to explore the intuitive excitement of the vocational option. You have discovered how important meaning, inspiration and a sense of "calling" are to the process of vocation development, so now you need to trust your inner voice to guide you to the vocational opportunities that seem the most exciting to you.

Five stars would literally get your soul stirring as you reflect on how amazing it would be to develop this vocation. Four stars would do the same, except that there might be a doubt that creeps into your mind about one particular aspect of this vocation. Three stars would mean that you are approaching indifference, and anything below that would suggest that the idea is not igniting any emotional fires. Try to gauge intuitively, even though you may have no experience in that specific vocational option.

Filter 2 – Long-term vocational journeys

Out of all the vocational options you have identified, some of them may have the following characteristics:

- Feel like a potentially big picture – the grand dream and the ultimate destination.
- Take significant amounts of time to fully work towards or achieve.
- Require extensive further study or financial investment.
- Feel the furthest out of your comfort zone.

The amazing thing about a Breakaway is that it affords the space to work on different vocations concurrently, or consecutively over a period of time. If you are a DJ, working towards your own record label or production studio would be an example of a top long-term vocational journey that really inspires you. It would get, say, four or five stars and get the reference "LT" in the next column (long term).

Short-term vocational projects

There may be vocational options that fit the following characteristics:

- An easy way to make quick money at home or on your travels.
- A seasonal opportunity relevant to a time of year.
- Require little development in terms of skills, but may require certification.

The whole point of a Breakaway is to gain experience. The reality, however, is that to fully explore something, we need the time and money to do so. Short-term vocational projects provide such a window. Even though they may not feel like vocations that will keep you fulfilled in the long term, they offer a very convenient way to make extra income. When someone has been a full-time professional, this list will also allow a critical shift in thinking. It will help one to identify how to apply individual skills in order to generate income during the transition to a more fulfilling long-term vocational journey.

Evaluate the value of the project with a mark out of five, and make the reference ST (short term).

Prioritising. Having completed this process, you now need to prioritise and rank all your top long-term vocational journeys and best short-term vocational projects. Copy and paste all the fives to the top, follow with the fours and then the threes. Anything below a three should not be taken over from the Career Constellation to your Vocational Dashboard.

If, having completed your Breakaway, you find yourself in the highly unlikely position in which not one of your top-ranked options was suitable, or you discovered nothing that felt meaningful on your trip, you can always try the ones that you initially ranked lower on your list. Rather discover this on work experience than after you have studied a degree in a subject for four years!

Use the highlighting function in Excel to give fives one colour, fours another colour and then finally, threes a different colour.

8

SURVIVAL OF THE FITTEST

GALAPAGOS ISLANDS

As I handed over a whole month's budget for an experience that was going to last only four days, I really doubted it would be worth it.

I knew of the Galapagos Islands from studying Charles Darwin and his journey to the archipelago as part of the famous Beagle voyage. It was here that the legendary biologist had the "Aha" moment that would contribute to his groundbreaking book that brought to life the theory of evolution and survival of the fittest: *On the Origin of Species*.

Despite being excited to be in the place where Darwin received his inspiration, the animal he had studied was the humble finch – a small bird that could not exactly be called a titan of the wildlife world. For someone who had grown up in South Africa observing elephants, lion and giraffe, the finch did not quite compete.

I was told that the islands had amazing sea life, but South Africa has the most nutrient-rich waters in the world. I had surfed with dolphins, observed humpback whales breeding and been submerged in a cage while diving with the awesome Great White shark. How the Galapagos could compete with South Africa, I was not sure.

I was travelling with Emma, who comes from the United Kingdom where the pinnacle of wildlife is foxes, hedgehogs, rabbits and the rest of the crew from Beatrix Potter stories. When I handed over the money for the trip, I have to admit that it was more for her than for me.

Arriving in Puerto Ayoro, the main port on Santa Cruz Island, we were greeted by turquoise-blue waters and the greedy cries of gulls swooping overhead. We booked ourselves on a four-day cruise on a boat called the Pelican. We would be visiting some of the most famous islands, including Sante Fe, Espanola, San Cristobal and Kicker Rock. With no idea of what to expect, we set sail from port, feeling like young explorers about to experience one of the planet's most isolated ecosystems.

It was not 10 minutes before the Galapagos began its show – and what a spectacle it was! First to greet us was a pod of about 50 dolphins, riding our boat's bow wave. They raced the vessel for more than 15 minutes, often jumping high into the air to our shrieks of delight. After what seemed like a well choreographed welcome performance, we were totally taken aback by the site of large manta rays doing back-flips out of the water as they hunted for prey.

This was followed by a lone turtle swimming casually past our boat as it came up for air. It was clear to me that we were indeed in a special place, yet the emerging difference was not how I felt about the environment, but how I felt about myself. This dichotomy would grow as the beauty of nature unfolded before us.

Whether we were floating with turtles; doing synchronised swim-ming with sea lions; staring down iguanas; or observing 100-year-old tortoises, the Galapagos kept taking our breath away. Just when we thought we had seen it all, another miracle of nature emerged.

Snorkelling between two giant pillars of rock in the middle of the ocean, we moved along the water's surface as literally dozens of sharks, including hammerheads and white tips, circled below. Even though we had no reason to feel afraid, it made me feel truly alive and vulnerable as a lone shark emerged stealthily from the darkness, looked me in the face and then carried on into the ocean void.

I marvelled at the body of this highly evolved killing machine. The shark's natural design, unchanged for almost two million years, had endured all of life's trials, resulting in the refined form that glided past me. Its sleek shape and fins allowed it to move effortlessly through the water, and its rapid speed and sharp teeth made it a lethal predator. It had adapted perfectly to its environment.

That shark was the product of literally millions of small adaptations that all species need to endure in order to survive. It was a reminder of how we need to adapt to our environment. Any species that does not adapt to its circumstances, simply disappears.

I was really happy to have Emma on the trip with me, not only because she had got me to commit to it, but because the Galapagos has to be one of the most romantic places in the world. While snorkelling together, we came across a turtle moving slowly across the bottom of the ocean. It allowed us to get so close that we could stare deep into the ancient reptile's eyes. The turtle then continued effortlessly, the sunlight silhouetting its form as we hovered above.

Gliding along hand-hand, in unison with the enchanted creature, Emma and I looked at each other. In that moment, we knew we were sharing something very special. It was one of the most peaceful and romantic moments of my life.

One of the most amazing things about the Galapagos – and what created this dichotomy in how I felt about myself – is that it has been so well protected that the animals do not fear humans. Tourists are only allowed to access 3% of the entire archipelago, and the park rangers ensure that you do not interfere with the balance of the ecosystem.

The result is a completely unique communion with nature in which the human is neither feared nor preyed upon. In an urban environment, a bird will normally raise hell if you get to close to its nest, but in the Galapagos, we were able to walk right up to giant albatrosses – the largest flying birds in the world – as they warmed their eggs and fed their young.

We had been taken closer to nature than we had ever been before, but we were also provided with some heart-breaking reminders of how brutal nature can be. This was most evident with the sea lions. We would find half-dead babies lying on the beach that had literally been squashed by the larger males. Such realities allowed us to engage with the fundamental truth that we are intrinsically connected to nature and to the cycles that dominate the living world. Other than life and death, one of the most fundamental of these cycles is change.

Adapting to change

Of all the organisms that have ever lived, almost 99.9% are extinct. They are dead because they could not adapt to their new environment. The ones that still survive, including us and the humble finch, have done so because they have transformed, learned and adapted, while enjoying a good amount of luck.

Humans are one of the most inventive and resilient species on the planet, yet we still struggle to adapt when life unfolds in unexpected ways. The catalyst that sparks a change or a new beginning may be very formal, like the end of schooling or university, or retirement from a professional career. It may be completely unexpected, like the loss of a loved one, poor health or being fired from one's job.

At the time of writing this book, the world is still reeling from the recession of 2008. One statistic I read in a newspaper in the United Kingdom suggested there were 46 graduates in the country competing for every single vacancy in 2013.[15] Every one of those graduates believed that by completing their degrees, following the conventional norms of society and relying on the economy to provide employment, they would be okay.

The reality is very different. Having been conditioned to believe that there will be a demand for their skills and that they can only add value in one arena, many people stand like dodos on a cliff edge, watching the winds of change tip their business models and career paths towards extinction.

Vocation development is about discovering a career that provides a real sense of meaning and purpose in the marketplace. It is our own El Dorado, the City of Gold, that provides us with a sense of adventure, personal significance and the promise of wealth.

Discovering one's vocation and building a sustainable career or business around one's own El Dorado is not easy. We need to develop skills, earn degrees and endure significant emotional insecurity as we invest money in starting up a new venture, or in the ever-increasing cost of education.

The implications of failure include massive debt, stress on family and partners, and potential ruin. Vocation development is a dangerous game. Considering the consequences, one would expect nothing short of absolute thoroughness and a survival-of-the-fittest mentality.

---

[15]   http://www.highfliers.co.uk/download/GMRelease13.pdf (accessed 5/8/2014)

Facing realities

The statistics around business failure are shocking. About 50 % of all businesses fail in the United States after five years.[16] In the United Kingdom, an average of one in three new businesses is still in operation after three years.[17] A business ultimately fails because it runs out of money, but one of the biggest reasons this happens is a lack of research. Understanding what people want and giving it to them does not sound that complicated, so you have to wonder why people go so far off course.

Imagine approaching the crash site of a business or a career failure and using forensic expertise to understand exactly what transpired. The narrative would start with the "victim" sitting on a glorious beach during a Breakaway, staring out into the expansive sea that serves as a perfect canvas for a new career plan.

We love these domains because they give us something that we crave more than anything – control. Through our intelligence, un-paralleled access to information and ability to learn, we believe we can foresee potential challenges, predict opportunities and brainstorm ideas that overcome concerns relevant to every scenario under the sun. There is no shortage of books to help us develop the skills and systems needed to create a new career.

What these faculties also provide – which is exactly where things start to go wrong – is pleasure. Slowly but surely, our analysis of the key problems we are trying to solve shifts to the fantasy of us getting it

---

[16]   United States Department of Commerce; Census Bureau; Business Dynamics Statistics: United States Department of Labour, Bureau of Labor Statistics, BED.

[17]   http://www.ons.gov.uk/ons/rel/bus-register/business-demography/2011/ stb-business-demography-2011.html (accessed 6/10/2014)

right: the joys of economic freedom; praise from our peers; and the diversity of a high-flying career.

It's time to test

The degree to which we test our assumptions during every stage of our process will influence the ultimate success of our new venture. The more we become attached to pleasurable outcomes related to success, the less we test and open ourselves to the probability that we could be wrong.

It is not always about moving towards pleasure. Often, it is about moving away from pain, in the form of anxiety and uncertainty. Remember, knowing what to do as a career can be major problem, and discovering innovative business ideas is not easy. When we find one that we think will work, we are often reluctant to consider that it won't work, lest we find ourselves lost and without purpose again. This is not an enjoyable space in which to be.

What's more, there is no shortage of self-help books that tell us that with the power of visualisation, affirmation and belief, we can create our own reality and overcome any obstacle. Any hint of doubt is considered to be weakness, and people becoming unwilling to accept any feedback that challenges their beliefs.

One of the greatest gifts of science is its strict regimen for testing hypotheses. When we dream up ideas for our career, we are developing our own hypotheses: *"I will enjoy this!"*; *"I will be good at this"*; *"This degree will get me a job"*; or *"This business is very lucrative"*. The first scientific experiment is always to test against the null – that is, to attempt to prove that your assumptions are false.

Unfortunately, we tend to make educated guesses on what is probable and not actually detectable through signals in the marketplace.

We then come up with solutions to every scenario that still supports an ultimate objective to which we have become emotionally attached. The drivers of that emotion could be acceptance from our parents, recognition from our peers, or the significance of having made it in a specific industry.

Race on your own track

The result is that as the wheels of our car start to skid, we focus on the ultimate goal hundreds of miles off in the distance, without really understanding why we are unable to hold the road just a few metres ahead.

Those people, excited about a new vocation, who then throw themselves into all types of degrees or business proposals without sufficient research and experience, can be likened to a skidding tyre that is expending huge amounts of energy without gaining traction. If such people only spent a bit more time understanding the surface on which they are driving, they would be able to perform optimally.

What makes things even more difficult is that we often feel we are in a race. Call it the rat race or the game of life, we are under huge pressure to reach the finish line, even though we may have forgotten or not known why we are even racing in the first place.

It is a big mistake to believe that we are all on the same track and that we are racing against each other. Often we compare our financial success, homes, relationships and progress on the corporate ladder to that of others. This pressure makes people rush into specific careers or tertiary degrees without allowing themselves the opportunity to experience or research different options. Parents who don't fully appreciate the value of a Breakaway can also apply pressure that leads to premature decisions; and financial pressure can prompt people to find jobs that satisfy short-term financial needs rather than a vocation.

The truth is that we are all on our own individual race track that has its own unique route, surface and conditions. We will encounter challenging corners and obstacles at different times of our journey. You may have to deal with a blind rise while a close friend is heading down their home straight.

Doing your research allows you to choose the tyres that will allow you the best opportunity to run your own race in the most fulfilling way. We all like to approach life at different speeds and will gain satisfaction from different aspects of the journey.

Research will allow you to find an innovation-driven link between your vocational aspirations and the needs of the marketplace. Innovation is vital. It will ultimately guarantee the survival of a vocation.

To keep us going on our personal journeys, we create inspiring visions of ourselves holding amazing jobs or owning innovative businesses, along with all of the benefits that come from such a life. With those inspiring visions come all of the emotional resilience we will need to keep going through the hard times. But when we create emotionally charged visions, we also tend to create expectations, and our driving force becomes the very thing that inhibits our ability to adapt to changing circumstances.

Many clients I have interviewed felt that expressing a sense of purpose through a vocation could be a huge source of disappointment to an individual, as not realising the goals that give one's life meaning can bring one's whole existence into question. Suddenly, we feel rejected, lost and insecure. We can see the door to our old lives and the safety of a secure job sitting easily in reach, yet we know that we have crossed the threshold.

* * *

I gave my three months' notice at Red Zebra in September 2008. In October, the global economy experienced the biggest crash since the Great Depression of 1929. I found myself facing the option to potentially withdraw my resignation and enjoy the safety of my job at Red Zebra until things blew over, or to brave the journey that I had been planning for more than a year.

I made the leap, and as I toasted the new Elixir business at my farewell at Red Zebra, I felt both excited and nervous that I would be journeying out on my own. In my bank was what I believed to be a solid cushion that would enable me to get my business off the ground. All I needed to do was follow through on the strategy that I had created by manifesting my vocational vision.

Almost six months down the line, my cash-flow had dwindled and things had started to feel confused. The uptake of my primary product, the nature-based experiences had been slow. I had not got the response I had anticipated. What's more, either out of curiosity or panic, I had tried to develop a few more products that, in my mind, could have appealed to a wider range of people. Soon what had been branded as a wilderness-based development company had developed into a fully-fledged consultancy that offered services to a wide range of industries.

In my confusion, I was scrambling to satisfy too many different needs and inspirations at the same time. Each new product required me to develop a new skill, to pilot a different process, and to gather the confidence and energy to take the product to a market in which I had significant passion, but ultimately no experience. I was trying to be everything to everybody, and I never really gained traction in any one specific area.

Eventually, my financial resources started to wear thin; I lost traction and headed for a crash. I had thrown myself into any market that seemed exciting. Had I spent more time gaining experience and researching vocations, I would have enjoyed a much smoother ride.

Your turn – The Research Cascade

Pool your options

Think of the cascade of water from a waterfall: a body of water flows over a precipice where, for a moment, it gets scattered in hundreds of directions by small rocks that shift its direction back into ever more concentrated streams. The liquid seems to flow effortlessly along the path of least resistance on its way down hundreds of little rocky steps, changing direction with rapid responsiveness.

The waterfall is a perfect metaphor for your Breakaway process. At the start, you are sitting on the edge, looking for a new direction, completely oblivious to where you will end up. You toss yourself out into the unknown and allow what feels like your whole body to be pulled apart, thrust in different directions and scattered.

However, trying to follow all of your vocational options to completion at the same time would be like spreading the mass of the cascade over a large surface and expecting it to still form a pool, or mass of any consequence. All of your enthusiasm, time and money would be wasted on several things that ultimately never make any impact. If you take that same energy and focus it in a very specific direction and at high pressure, you will find the ability to crack rock with awesome power.

Experimentation and research can be equated to the cascade. We are all on a different career journey, and at each junction there are thought leaders, organisations and mentors who, like rocks, provide us with subtle clues as to the path of least resistance. Remember, waterfalls have been cutting through mountains for millennia. Sometimes the change in energy and direction of the water is so powerful that it causes the river to burst its banks and create whole new streams.

Successful career-builders are often labelled as lucky, or as being in the right place at the right time. What people don't realise is the preparation that got those people into the positions in which they could take advantage of those opportunities. You can be sure that like water, they were open to the signals from the rocks of their industry and they were changing their direction way before any chance of getting stuck.

These rocks are touchstones of experience that provide us with important information. At every juncture, we have the ability to change our direction, based on experiences that are either unfulfilling, or that reinforce that we are on the right path. When we consider that a cascade often involves hundreds of little changes of direction before the river evens out into a steady flow, we need to remain fluid. However, don't expect that if you have found your stream, it will remain tranquil all the way to the ocean. Know that you will be thrust back into a cascade as you navigate changes in your journey.

On our journey, we may also come across puddles of water that have somehow been cut off from the main river. Without life and movement, the water grows murky and stagnant. Being stubborn, fearful and unwilling to learn, or just staying in the same place, can lead to stagnancy. We may find ourselves stuck or unable to break through into new territory because we don't have enough momentum behind us. Many entrepreneurs or career builders develop innovative products that the market is just not ready for.

But, as you set out on your journey, trust that the rocks will guide you to your ultimate destination.

Rock 1: Thought leaders

A thought leader is a person who shapes the vocation in which you are interested. It may be someone who works in a prestigious academic institution, or a person who is dominating the front pages of the global business media.

Meeting with a thought leader will give you access to an unparalleled level of experience and understanding, as well a network of resources to take your vocation forward. In a matter of hours, a thought leader could potentially save you years of hard learning, exorbitant education expenses and wasted time.

Some thought leaders will have global reputations, while others will have demonstrated significant leadership in your home city. It is important to identify both types of thought leaders. It is usually easier to first connect to the local ones. There is a good chance that once you have built a relationship with them, they will be happy to refer you to all manner of experienced people.

Being at the top of their game, they will also be able to give you insight into what it is like at the top, including the benefits and the sacrifices that will need to be made. They can also share their vision for the future of your shared vocation.

People often develop mentor relationships with thought leaders. If you have identified someone who shares your passions, values and even perhaps your abilities, it is likely that you will develop significant rapport with this person.

"You remind me of when I was starting out" is a classic example of someone finding meaning in the journey of another, and enjoying a sense of legacy that allows you to carry forward the flame of your shared passion.

Every person wants to leave a legacy of some kind because, in many ways, we fear our mortality. Keeping a part of ourselves alive through the next generation gives us a sense of meaning. You are that next generation in your vocation and you should never deny someone the opportunity to create a legacy by giving you the gift of their experience, wisdom and energy. Just don't believe you are entitled to it!

Rock 2: Industry leaders

In every industry there is a company or organisation that leads from the front – a company that takes the industry forward through innovation; customer service; corporate social investment and even by providing the best work environment.

While you are gaining experience, you may still have no idea whether you want to start your own business or whether you want to be an employee. Either way, it makes sense to gain experience with the best of the best. Not only will it give you a snapshot of what things are like at the pinnacle of an industry, but if you then decide you want to work in that industry, you would have already built a relationship and have had a chance to demonstrate some value to the best company in your field.

The industry leader is not always the biggest or the oldest in the game. In fact, such leaders are often boutique companies that recognise that size brings complexity that prevents innovation.

Rock 3: Industry associations

Most established industries have associations, like the Professional Golf Association or the Automobile Association. They are organisations that represent the collective interests of all stakeholders involved in a specific industry. An association will have relationships with all of the

BREAKAWAY

key roleplayers and should have a good understanding of the opportunities and challenges facing the industry as a whole. It will also have an intimate knowledge of who the thought and industry leaders are. They will organise conferences, exhibitions and association meetings where these movers and shakers will be invited to participate.

The association will also have relationships with other roleplayers in the economy, such as government, the Reserve Bank and associations from other countries. It is in their interests to manage these relationships, because actions from any one of these players can mean significant consequences for their industry as a whole. If you want to gain experience in a new industry, associations are great connections to make.

Connecting to your rocks: Six degrees of separation

So, how do you gain access to these people, organisations and associations? Surely if they are a thought or industry leader and you have no relationship with them whatsoever, there is a slim chance of them giving you the time of day in their busy schedules – particularly if you have no clear value proposition for them, other than gaining experience?

In the earlier chapters we spoke about the importance of tribes to the safety of each individual. In a dangerous and uncertain world, you could count on your tribe members for safety, compassion and support.

Strangers were regarded as potential competitors, thieves and even threats to the safety of the members. Any newcomer who approached the tribe had to do so with huge caution and it took a significant amount of time and energy to build trust and confidence.

Today, things are no different. Although there are numerous vehicles through which we can connect to potential new members of

118

our tribe, when it comes to serious issues, like work and relationships, we regard strangers with significant suspicion -unless they are referred to us by one of our own tribe members.

The referral is the most powerful relationship-building catalyst in all areas of our lives. When buying new products; starting intimate relationships or finding a job, referrals through friends and organisations come up trumps every time.

Friends are the primary introducers of couples of all types (35–40%).[18] Research studies indicate that 40–50% of people secure their jobs through contacts.[19] People are, on average, seven times more likely to get business if a friend or family member reviews a product than through a celebrity endorsement.[20]

We spend ages approaching companies through job pages and recruitment companies, although companies will first welcome people recommended through their network of employees. New entrepreneurs spend huge amounts of money advertising in industry publications, although someone in their circle of friends is probably connected to the CEO of potentially their biggest client. We always underestimate networking!

Everyone says the world is getting smaller, yet we still treat each other as complete strangers and forget the fact that at one time, the

---

[18] *Hearts and Minds: How Our Brains Are Hardwired for Relationships*, Thomas David Kehoe, Casa Futura Technologies, 2003

[19] *Networking, Not Internet Cruising, Still Lands Most Jobs for Those in Career Transition*, Monika Morrow, SVP Career Management Services – Americas, Right Management. May 8 2013; http://www.right.com/blog/talentpluswork/2013/networking-not-internet-cruising-still-lands-most-jobs-for-those-in-career-transition/

[20] http://www.harrisinteractive.com/vault/HI-Harris-Poll-Opinions-In-Social-Media-2010-06-03.pdf (accessed 6/10/2014)

population of the world numbered no more than a 100 000 people and that we all used to live in the same area.

We all descend from this core group of early humans and we remain connected. The fact that there are now six billion people in the world probably intimidates many, yet we forget that we are related to every person on the planet by no more than six degrees of separation.

The theory works on the premise that every person in the world is no more than six links away from you. There are anomalies, like Amazonian tribes, but if you are connected to the information super-highway, your ability to connect with people to whom you are related is significant.

"Related" does not necessarily have to mean a family connection. It includes work, friendship, community or interests. Irrespective of where the connection is, the important thing is that when you approach the person, you are not simply some stranger at the tribal boundary.

Services like LinkedIn and Facebook have allowed us to make these connections in a powerful way. We can now consider almost every person on the planet as a fellow tribe member. If we approach them in the right way, we can access almost any opportunity within any organisation that is driven by any thought leader. According to statisticians, if you are on Facebook, the degrees of separation can drop to as low as four.[21]

With enough patience and strategic thought, one can always narrow down the strongest connections to a specific thought leader. Although you may share the same passions and values as this person and have a connection to them, you may also be conscious of the fact that there

---

[21]   *Four Degrees of Separation*, L. Backstrom, P. Boldi, M. Rosa, J. Ugander, S. Vigna, Association for Computing Machinery Press,

are hundreds of others trying to spend time with them. It is important that you know how to proceed.

Gaining access to your thought leader or organisation

Accessing the greatest minds in the world means having to compete against many other people, so this is where the game really heats up and demands your mental and social resilience.

You may have already had a negative experience while trying to engage with a thought leader. Perhaps, when you made contact, you received no feedback whatsoever. Maybe you engaged with the super-courteous personal assistant who, no matter how nice they were trying to be, always had the undertone of: "Who are you?" You have probably been reminded that the thought leader receives 400–500 new emails each day. It may have then been explained to you that they receive all kinds of requests, and even if the leader quit their job and focused on their email full time, it would still be a while before they got back to you.

So, how do you access that person quickly? How do you get your name to jump out when they go through their inbox? How do you get them to respond?

- **Have a well-researched reason for contacting them.**
  Be very clear about the result that you want to achieve from your contact with this person. It must be some inspiration or a piece of information that you can't get anywhere else other than through a face-to-face conversation, phone call or email. Imagine chasing a thought leader for many weeks. You finally get your chance to ask them something, only to have them respond that the answer is on their company's home page. Your thought leader would view you as

121

someone who does not do their homework and does not appreciate their time. Be prepared for the interaction.

- **Go in with an attitude of service and giving.**

  Most thought leaders have developed a gift and purpose that allows them to make an empowered contribution to the world. When this gift is of significant value, people often demand it ruthlessly. Thought leaders have to balance the needs of their careers; fans; media; foundations; businesses; and their friends and family, who all want a piece of their time and energy. To cope with these demands, they develop what seems to be an impenetrable shield to any distractions that could impact on their time. There is a reason personal assistants are called gatekeepers – they are the ones who guard the thought leaders' time.

  Most people mistakenly only make contact when they want something from a thought leader. When this leader has enhanced your life through a book you have read, or through an experience they have organised, tell them straight away. Call them; demonstrate that appreciation with a little gift or a meaningful account of your transition. What's more, try to do it in a creative way so that your gratitude stands out as an expression of your innovative capabilities.

  Slowly, you will start to build a relationship with this person, and the chance of them helping you in the future increases. Instead of them regarding you as just another demanding person, on future occasions when your name pops up, they could view you as a source of appreciation, gratitude and giving. When you do finally need something from them, the chances of them helping you increase significantly.

- **Care about the industry, the product and the people.**

  It is one thing to express a passion for a product or industry, it is quite another to contribute towards its development. A company or thought leader gives their time and energy to regular customers because, after all, they are the reason they are in business, and they want to show reciprocity. Your ability to access them will improve dramatically when you go from being a passive consumer to an active catalyst in the industry, irrespective of what position you hold.

  If you are really inspired to contribute to a company you are passionate about, you will engage on company forums; write letters of complaint or praise; involve yourself in customer focus groups; attend expos; and blog about your experiences. If you find yourself struggling to do these things, then you have to question your real motives for building relationships with these companies and exploring the vocation in the first place. This is a great thing to test on your Breakaway.

  If you were passionate about the art of investing, you would seize any opportunity to learn from Warren Buffett. Just by investing in the stock market, the Oracle of Omaha turned $10 000 in 1960 into a personal fortune of more than $70 billion today.[22]

  Gaining access to this thought leader is not easy. However, if you owned Berkshire Hathaway stock, you would be invited to the annual company conference where you would have an opportunity to connect with Buffett. He makes himself available to investors because he knows that without the people who buy into his company, the organisation would not exist or grow.

---

[22] http://www.forbes.com/profile/warren-buffett/ (accessed 7/10/2014)

Several years ago, attendees at a charity auction were able to bid for the opportunity to have lunch with Buffett. The record payment to the charity was $3.8 million. If you think this was simply an expression of generosity, think again. The advice that Buffett could give in an afternoon could be worth even more than the amount paid for the opportunity. The following year, a fund manager named Ted Weschler won the bid with a donation of $2.8 million. He was later employed by Buffett. He had made such a significant contribution to Buffett's charity that it became almost impossible for Buffett to not practice reciprocity.

- **When you speak from the heart, people listen.**
By developing a bold plan for a business, a Breakaway or even a career, you create a powerful vision with the expectation of success and fulfilment. Having identified that an opportunity to gain experience from a specific thought leader is critical to the realisation of that vision, it may be that you place a lot of pressure and importance on your engagement with them. This creates significant opportunities for fear and desperation to creep in. This will dramatically impact on how you interact with that person.

You may feel the need to impress them in the hope that they will recognise some brilliance in you that will compel them to help you further. Often, though, things can swing to the other extreme, where we transform from being empowered purpose-driven leaders into orphans crying out from the curb of mediocrity.

The world needs and responds to an open heart and sheer inspiration. No matter what level of experience you have in a specific area, your heart reveals your passion and how it serves humanity. When you speak from this place, your congruency is at its highest and you achieve a level of integrity that immediately grabs people's attention. When you align your vision with that of a thought leader, based on principle rather than status, there is a level of rapport that binds you together in a collective mission.

Following the path of least resistance

Explore all of your vocations through the cascade

If you do not follow a clear research strategy, it is possible to make the following critical mistakes:

- Taking a job before you have had the opportunity to fully experience all the vocations in which you are interested. If you identify 10 vocations and then take a job after experiencing only the first, how can you ever be sure you have fully explored your options?

- Enrolling in expensive or time intensive degrees or certifications without any clear idea of return on investment or how much you will enjoy related careers. The same can be said of risking money when starting a business.

- Ruining an opportunity for experience or employment by overselling yourself before you have identified where you can add value. Experience is not about forcing yourself into opportunities. Rather, it is about embracing the power that comes from a patient, incremental and thorough strategy.

After coaching clients for a number of years and having conducted my own experiment on my Breakaway, I can offer you a logical process that will ensure that you manage the "experience journey" effectively. The following structure will support you and help you overcome the following limiting beliefs:

- I have to quit my job to gain experience.
- I cannot get experience without a significant financial cushion.
- I can only research one vocation at a time.

Cascade Level 1

Internet research

There are many internet resources to help you explore the nature of a given vocation or industry. Even though you are exploring, be very clear about the general information you are seeking for each vocational option.

Ease of access: Easy.

Cost of access: Free or nominal internet costs.

Time commitment: You can research for as long as you need to do it, but don't get lost in the process! Be very specific about the information you need.

Value to you in terms of experience: Theoretical.

Quality of information: General, related to each vocational option.

Disruption to your current responsibility: Very limited.

Cascade Level 2

Coffee or lunch

This is not to be underestimated for its ability to create the space for you to gain brief and inexpensive access to a thought leader, as well as information related to a vocational option. It also allows you to practice reciprocity by gifting the person with lunch in exchange for their time.

Ease of access: Easy. Everyone has to eat.

Cost of access: Easily affordable. Unless it's a Warren Buffet charity auction.

Time commitment: 20 minutes to two hours.

Value to you in terms of experience: Insight into a person's professional journey, opportunities in an industry and referrals to other thought leaders and organisations. Still theoretical.

Quality of information: Relevant to one profession in an industry.

Disruption to your current responsibilities: Very limited.

Cascade Level 3

Attend networking events or industry association meetings

All professionals go to networking meetings. Whether it's a breakfast meeting at your local chamber of commerce, or a specialised association conference, it is always better to engage with people when they are open to new ideas, engaging with strangers and prepared to network.

Ease of access: General access or referral through your coffee contact.

Cost of access: Easily affordable, to free.

Time commitment: One to two hours, usually out of office hours.

Value to you in terms of experience: Insight into professional journeys; more opportunities in the industry; and even more referrals to other thought leaders and organisations. Still theoretical.

Quality of information: A wide variety of viewpoints from professionals in one industry, or several. An understanding of the needs of the profession and the consumer.

Disruption to your current responsibilities: Very limited.

Cascade Level 4

Industry conferences and exhibitions – national and local

Every industry has the one conference that is its true commercial hub, both locally and globally. All of the key players will be concentrated in one area: thought leaders; suppliers; consumers; key decision-makers; innovators; law-makers; employers; and entrepreneurs. For anyone who is looking to explore a new industry and the professions it supports, you could never ask for a better space to do it than a leading expo or conference.

Ease of access: Easy for exhibitions and general conferences.

Cost of access: Fees can be expensive for global industry-leading conferences or expos. Could be cheaper for a local event.

Time commitment: One to two days during week for conference and expo's on the weekend.

Quality of experience to you: Insight into the whole industry and a significant number of new contacts. An ability to understand the needs of the industry as a whole. Still theoretical.

Quality of information: A wide variety of viewpoints from professionals in one industry, or several. An understanding of the needs of the profession and the consumer.

Disruption to your current responsibilities: You may need to take a day's leave to attend a conference during the week. Expos are usually held over weekends. Sometimes these events happen once a year so don't let this slow down your ability to do observational days or get work experience. They are a nice to have not a have to have.

Cascade Level 5

Observational days

My father decided he wanted to study medicine. Having completed six months of theoretical study, he was faced with his first practical:

dissecting a frog. He was so put off by the experience that he changed his degree to law. When exploring the notion of being a doctor, my father could have saved a whole year of study by just spending a few days observing the fundamental nature of the profession he was pursuing. Whether it is sitting in the cockpit of a plane, spending a weekend on the road with a rock band, or taking in the dynamics of a trading floor in a bank, just go in and get a taste of the profession you are considering.

Ease of access: Easy – observation provides no disruption to an organisation's workflow.

Cost of access: Free to you and to the company.

Time commitment: One to three days.

Quality of experience to you: Observational experience is much more valuable than theoretical research. Ability to build contacts in the whole organisation and to understand specific needs of the organisation.

Disruption to your current responsibilities: Need to take a few days' leave, or build it into your Breakaway.

Cascade Level 6

Work experience

Work experience is about involving yourself in the actual work of your profession. You cannot get a proper feel for a potential vocation until you have embodied the experience. If you want to be a journalist, that might mean writing an article. If you are keen to be an architect, build a model and do some drawings. Spend time doing the actual work demanded of your profession. You cannot do work experience by just observing, as many school programmes and organisations suggest.

Ease of access: Medium difficulty – requires allocation of employee's time and energy.

Cost of access: Free, but loss of time to the company.

Time commitment: One to two weeks.

Quality of experience to you: Actual work experience.

Disruption to your current responsibilities: You do not necessarily have to be in the organisation to experience the work. Write articles or build architectural models from home. However, you will more than likely need to take time off to properly experience an organisation.

Cascade Level 7

Internships, mentorships and apprentices

After you have had a few observational days and some actual work experience, only then should you consider an internship. Internships are either formalised or ad hoc experience programmes in which employers can evaluate the suitability, positioning and further skill requirements of the candidate. Companies will only consider taking on a person for an internship if they have one of the following:

- The minimum educational requirements and certificates.
- A demonstration of passion and raw talent that will quickly add value through in-house training.

Ease of access: Difficult – requires allocation of employee's time and energy over a longer period.

Cost of access: Money required to live, if not being paid a full stipend.

Time commitment: One to three months.

Quality of experience to you: Closest to being employed, with un-rivalled access to industry, company and employees.

Disruption to your current responsibilities: Requires a significant window of time.

As has become evident, there is a very logical and conscious process to exploring potential vocations. It is the path of least resistance. The only time that some form of education, whether it be a certificate or a particular degree, is absolutely necessary, is when one is doing an internship. Even then, it is possible for people to become apprentices by showing enough passion and talent. Relationships are often the key.

Intuition is so important when it comes to vocational development, and at each stage of this process you are getting a feel for a vocational option before committing more time and energy to the next stage.

Still sticking to our strategy of using our network, you can see how much easier it is for someone to refer you from one stage of the research strategy to the next. You are also in the best position to maximise your number of contacts, access to experience opportunities and the chance to understand the needs of an industry through thought leaders and leading companies.

Now, let's add another layer to your Vocational Dashboard.

Stage of experience

On your Breakaway you have the opportunity to complete a full research strategy for several potential vocations at the same time. This framework allows you to establish where you are currently sitting on an experience level, with all of the ideas, career options and industries that form part of your Dashboard. If you are heading out on your Breakaway, there may be several vocational options that you have yet to experience. They may be new interests or an amateur passion you have been developing that could still become a profession. You already may be at a more advanced stage of experience with another option. Add another column to your Vocational Dashboard with the title **Research Cascade**. Next to each vocational option, write down your stage of experience, and as you go through the cascade as you prepare for and engage in your Breakaway, change each stage. As soon as something does not feel right, divert energy into a new stream. Before you know it, you will have followed the path of least resistance to your vocation.

Here are the stages:
1. Still to be experienced
2. General research on the internet.
3. Coffee or lunch with thought leaders.
4. Attend networking events or industry association meetings.
5. Industry conferences and exhibitions – national and local – if convenient.
6. Observational days in leading organisations, if convenient.
7. Work experience in leading organisations.
8. Internships, mentorships and apprentices.

SLUMDOG LAWYERS, PROFESSORS AND DOCTORS

Emboldened by my relationships within the township communities of South Africa, I wasn't intimidated by the slums of Brazil. Admittedly, though, recalling the glaring eyes of the psychotic drug dealer, Little Z, in the movie *City of God* made me a little jumpy – as did the unexpected scream of a child.

As I entered a narrow cement corridor, I was greeted by a stench of sewerage and the faint chatter of people in their homes. It reminded me that life teemed here in the maze of Rio de Janeiro's favelas. It was 2012, and I was under the watch of a new friend who had felt confident enough to bring me into these notorious communities that had recently been "pacified" by the government ahead of the Soccer World Cup and in preparation for the 2016 Rio Olympics.

These favelas used to be self-contained fortresses that, despite a significant drug trade, had non-existent crime levels. Inhabitants went about their lives, safe in the knowledge that protecting the drug dealers guaranteed them a safe community. The leadership maintained vantage points over the whole slum, while a network of spotters and messengers flew kites that alerted the drug ring to the presence of the police or rival gangs. No strangers had previously been allowed in, and up until a year before my visit, it was unheard of for tourists to enter the area.

Riding in the new cable car that took us straight up to the throne of the previous leadership, I saw a large building at the top of the hill. Once guarded by youths with machine guns, I walked inside it without any trouble, only to discover a judo class underway in what had become the community centre.

Standing on the hill of the favela, overlooking the very township where Michael Jackson had filmed his 1992 music video *They Don't Care About Us*, I was struck by how things had moved on and opened up to outside influences. My friend pointed out where a group of Dutch volunteers had begun painting the drab shanty houses in bright colours. It was a reflection of the new life that was being breathed into these areas.

I was curious about how this world was going to change, now that these townships, ghettos or slums, were becoming the focus of various key roleplayers. One billion people currently live in these communities, and this figure is expected to grow to two billion by 2030. To entrepreneurs, these vibrant settlements represent a whole new marketplace, culture and way of living that is set to challenge the way in which the developed world views progress.

Staring at the young children running about the favela, I reflected on my own country and its battle to keep kids in schools without losing them to street gangs. Both countries face the age-old challenge of guiding children towards opportunities and preparing them accordingly.

But, how do you engage and educate a young man who drops out of school at the age of 14; becomes a drug lord who trades in 10 favelas; earns close to $200 000 a week; employs more than 200 soldiers; and has enough power to end a person's life in an instant? That was the story of Wandson, the leader of a drug ring. He had an average life expectancy of 25.

Wandson wanted to escape his perilous situation, but lacked any formal education. The state education system in Brazil – a country with one of the highest income inequality rates in the world – could not promise him a job and an income years down the line. If he was even lucky enough to get a job after receiving a formal education, it might not be sufficient to feed his starving family, or to compete with the overwhelming influence of the gangs.

Luckily, Wandon met a man named Rodrigo Baggio, who founded CDI, the Centre for Digital Inclusion. The organisation seeks to democratise access to IT and to engage people like Wandson long enough to educate them in practical technical skills that will provide them with opportunities that they can access immediately.

Most countries, including Brazil, still subscribe to the Bismarkian model that was developed in Germany in the 19th century. This system promises success and employment years down the line – if one learns vast quantities of information. However, much of this information is not relevant to someone who is simply trying to survive in a slum for one more day.

Because of the extreme circumstances in which they work, educators in the slums are at the cutting edge of their profession. They know that they have to teach information that adds value to the person's world today. More importantly, they have to be creative in the manner in which they capture young people's attention and interest. Any learning experience that is not relevant, exciting and based specifically on their values, could send the youths back to the dangerous world of drug dealing.

High unemployment rates around the world, especially among the youth, suggest that besides the normal scapegoat of the recession, there is a stark contrast between the skills that are being demanded by the rapidly changing market and those that are still being developed in schools that are struggling to adapt.

Traditionally, developed countries have cascaded teachings from the higher echelons of their education systems down to the poorest countries. Necessity is the mother of invention, and in these brutal economic times, professors from Harvard and Oxford are being challenged by education techniques that are emerging from the slums of Calcutta and Rio. Never before has there been a greater democratisation of learning, or such a need to overhaul conventional curricula in order to prepare young people for a chaotic future.

I am Jewish, so I fully appreciate the pressure of following a traditional route into a specific profession, such as law or medicine. My father turned to law from medicine after realising that the blood he wanted to draw was figurative rather than literal.

But, why the obsession with law and medicine? Before the age of the entrepreneur, professionals were held in the highest esteem. They kept you alive and on the right side of the law, so it was only fitting that they demanded the highest wages and attracted the sharpest minds – both Jew and gentile alike. A career in law or medicine was a gateway to social status, financial freedom and a comfortable life.

To become a professional, one had to follow the education paths endorsed by the associations that guaranteed best practice and industry standards. People endured years of study and were willing to take on significant student debt because they trusted the system and felt there was no other way to gain access to these prestigious professions.

But, just as the teachers in the slums of Brazil are bringing change to education, so too are poorer communities challenging other established professions and the education paths that are required to access them.

According to *The Economist*, in 2012, Britain had 27.4 doctors to every 10 000 patients. India had only six![23] The fact that there are just not enough doctors to meet the need in India means that hospitals have been forced to think outside of the box in order to meet the basic minimum requirement in the shortest amount of time. The result is that surgeries cost less than $2 000 each, about one-fifteenth as much as a similar surgery in America.

What with the juxtaposition of the expensive, regulated and entrenched associations in the developed economies, and the anything-goes attitude to innovation that is being practised in the poorest parts of the world, it is inevitable that we will see a radical shift in how people are trained and in what they earn in prestigious professions.

According to *The Financial Times*: "The Tesco Law that was implemented by the Labour Government of the United Kingdom in 2011 was to make legal work, such as will writing or conveyancing, as accessible and easy for consumers as buying a can of beans from a supermarket".[24] A highly educated aristocrat in a wig with a seven-year legal education could soon be replaced by a community college graduate in a Sainsbury's golf shirt with a three-month certificate in intellectual property law.

The most glamorous and romantic profession has to be that of a pilot. The sight of a pilot walking through a departure lounge wearing

---

[23] http://www.economist.com/node/21556227 (accessed 7/10/2014)

[24] http://www.ft.com/cms/s/0/6414f054-de1d-11e0-a115-00144feabdc0.
html#axzz3EGDY3RTH (accessed 7/10/2014)

a slick uniform, followed by a host of beautiful flight attendants, still tends to fill people with awe. There was a time when air travel was "the" luxury experience, and being a pilot was one of the most exciting and well-paid careers to which a young person could aspire. The education and training was gruelling and expensive. Besides the cost of doing tests and simulations, one had to pay for literally hundreds of hours of flight time before upgrading to commercial airliners.

In 2013, John Goglia, professor at Vaughn College of Aeronautics and Technology, reported that some entry level pilots were taking home less than McDonalds trainees after paying back the loans they had taken out for their own training.[25]

Yes, it will be a long time before professions like doctors, lawyers and pilots lose their hold on the collective psyche, but prized professions are no longer a given. In reality, people's perceptions of how lucrative a career is going to be, and the fees they are prepared to pay for an education, do not match up. Trends in various countries suggest a gradual decline in pay, adjusted for inflation, across the board in law, medicine and aviation.

Beware of parents' advice. They may be influencing you to spend significant amounts of time and energy to study a profession that could be obsolete in several years' time.

* * *

As I developed my Elixir business and started to explore the skills that I needed in order to solve my clients' challenges, I was overwhelmed by my choices. Besides the traditional business schools that offered large-

---

[25]   http://www.forbes.com/sites/johngoglia/2013/07/31/what-do-entry-level-regional-pilots-and-mcdonalds-workers-have-in-common/ (accessed 7/10/2014)

scale certifications, I could partake in a Mass Open Online Course (MOOC) which offered me a certification in a truly awesome array of subjects.

At the click of a mouse, I could complete a four-week course in Concepts in Game Development, hosted by Swinbourne University in Australia. As part of the development of this book, perhaps a 20 week course: A Brief History of Humankind, hosted by the Hebrew University of Jerusalem, would have been beneficial.

I discovered that I was able to do a 15-week course in language, proof and logic from Stanford University – one of the most prestigious universities in the world. It was being offered for free and provided a certificate at the end of an exam.

Why would the most prestigious universities in the world offer free courses? This is a matter of both necessity and choice. As more students find themselves working in jobs that don't require a degree, accompanied by a growing realisation that a college education does not guarantee employment, people are becoming more selective about how they choose their education.

The laws of supply and demand dictate the true price of an education. Acknowledging that the internet could potentially provide young people with the same skills at a vastly reduced rate, universities have begun to realise that they need to understand the true value of their degrees in monetary terms.

Proponents of university degrees have always claimed that acquiring a university degree provides a much better return on investment over time. New data from the Economic Policy Institute in Washington DC suggests that a graduate from an American university could expect an hourly wage that is 98% more than someone who went to another form of college.[26] Note that there is a difference between university and other colleges, and several studies suggest that graduate salaries are still rising.

This increase in wages is confusing, because a graduate salary is normally a function of demand. Understanding how we can have rising graduate salaries together with rising youth unemployment is a mystery. UCAS, the university clearing system in the UK, recorded a record volume of applications in 2014. It is clear that there is a lack of communication between employers and educators. All things being equal, if there was adequate communication between employers and educational institutions around the skills required from students, there would be falling unemployment.

No matter what people say about the actual value of the skills acquired through a degree, the unspoken value of attending both a quality university and school is the network and the reputation that comes with it. An Ivy League university insignia still represents an unparalleled opportunity to develop a network that improves employability; the ability to fund future endeavours by drawing on a potentially bigger pool of investors with whom you have some form of connection; and it provides a greater awareness of new opportunities as well as reputation. More than anything else, that is what people pay for.

The reason that universities, which are still getting solid application rates and enjoying rising fees, are embracing the e-learning revolution is that in time, they foresee a shift in the attitudes of both employers and students. As employers start to gain confidence in e-learning, they

---

[26] http://www.epi.org/publication/class-of-2013-graduates-job-prospects/ (accessed 7/10/2014)

will be prepared to take on students who do not graduate from these traditional, expensive institutions. A large portion of the wages that young graduates demand from companies goes to paying off the costs of their education. If employers eventually felt the same level of confidence in employing someone who is willing to accept half the salary because his education cost half that a traditional degree, you can be sure they would do so.

At the same time, students who rely less and less on the conventional approach to education and employment will start to experiment with new forms of learning. Instead of believing that a four year degree is the one-stop-shop to professional credibility, they will apply a much more targeted approach, using specific skills to add value to current situations. As e-learning becomes more popular, courses will produce graduates who will achieve huge success and fly the flag of the new learning revolution.

At the end of 2014, Emily-Rose Eastop, from the United Kingdom, used a global crowdfunding platform to get people to fund her course in cognitive and evolutionary anthropology at the University of Oxford. She had already completed her undergraduate at Oxford and earned a 2:1. She thought it would be easy to find a job, but four years later, she was still unemployed and sitting with more than £20 000 in debt.

Eastop then decided to do a postgraduate degree, again at Oxford. Unable to afford the extra £26 000 required for her studies, she hit a dead end. Seeing how many other people were able to fund a range of start-up ideas and projects through online platforms, such as Kickstarter and Hubbab, she was the first to ask the question: Why not get the people who value my degree to fund my formal education?

Her campaign resulted in her being labelled as a "posh spoilt brat", and some people saw it as a "distasteful form of modern begging".

Others were horrified that she had the nerve to think she could fund her education in any other way than a loan, or payments by her parents. Some people, who do not understand crowd funding, thought there were more deserving charities that should get their donation.

What people fail to appreciate about crowd funding is that people have to create real incentives in order for people to fund them. Only 40% of campaigns on Kickstarter are successful, so the emphasis is on convincing potential funders that they and the investment community will benefit from the proposal. Eastop offered to share the learnings from her degree with people who took an interest in science, cognition, and evolutionary anthropology. She provided subscriptions to her science blog, which already had more than 80 000 subscribers. To the largest funders, she offered a signed copy of her dissertation. This was enough to persuade people like Douglas Hofstadter and Stephen Pinker, both leaders in cognitive science and potential future employers, to fund her studies.

Crowd funding could be the very mechanism that allows employers and students to communicate more effectively around the skills they require to achieve current strategic objectives, and what they are prepared to pay for it. Why should students take on all the financial risk of getting a degree that they are not even sure that employers will need? Through crowd funding, they can approach the very people who need the skills and create a deal that involves real value exchange.

The development of incentives requires an understanding of the current value of what the student will learn; who will value that knowledge; what they will use that knowledge for; and, more importantly, how much they will be prepared to pay for it. Such platforms provide immediate monetary feedback around what the market values. If the potential student is unsuccessful in raising the money, they will know with much more certainty that perhaps the degree that they wish to study could become redundant, or is not worth the fees charged.

Slowly, e-learning platforms like MOOCS, and crowd-funding mechanisms such as Kickstarter, are going to strip away the largess that has accumulated, thanks to people relying on and paying for an outdated education that always guaranteed opportunity, no matter what you studied. The communication gap between strategic executives in large companies and the students required to develop the skills, will become smaller. We are experiencing the natural evolution of education as it comes to terms with huge changes in the global economy.

Your turn – Understand the costs

Part of an effective Breakaway is about understanding the various strategies and cost requirements of education in a specific vocation. This may be an MBA, a degree, or some other qualification. Not every person who has become successful attended a prestigious university or completed a must-have degree.

A Breakaway also involves stepping away from conventions and exploring the other ways in which one can gain the skills required to start practising a vocation straight away. This incremental approach saves money and ensures that you don't waste time studying a degree for a career that is not ultimately where you want to be. Let's not forget that education is also a business – one that is under threat from the internet.

Many people have no training whatsoever and have, with tenacity, networked their way into a job by expressing such raw talent and passion for a vocation that professionals have agreed to mentor, apprentice and even fund them.

The only way to understand the most cost-effective routes of gaining entry into a specific vocation is by building relationships with the people who are at its forefront. You will have identified these people in the previous chapter and while you are on your Breakaway.

Add another column to your Vocational Dashboard. Label it **Education**.

As you progress on your Breakaway, you are going to note all of the different paths that people took to access a specific vocation. The options will range from very formalised ones, like a degree, to free online tutorials.

As you come to the end of your Breakaway, you should have a very clear idea of the time and financial costs of pursuing different paths towards your specific vocation.

10

RISE OF THE MACHINES

had come a long way to reach this fabled road. For many seeking fame and glory, walking down this historic street lined with golden stars was a symbol of a dream. Thousands of aspiring actors, singers and producers flock to Hollywood each year clinging to ideas of fame, only to find fantasies of glamour and stardom shattered, as they end up waiting tables in restaurants and bars, rather than commanding the sets of the big film studios.

I was under no such illusions. As part of my Breakaway, I had experimented with writing a film script, which now sits covered in digital cobwebs in the depths of my computer. I had come to Hollywood on a much more sacred mission.

As I frantically scrambled along the walk, looking for the brightest star in my Hollywood sky, I could not contain my excitement. He had been my hero growing up and represented a time when action movies were all about cheesy one-liners, body counts in the hundreds, and martial arts moves that brought a tear to the eye. Jean Claude Van Damme had his helicopter kick; Steven Segal could take down 30 people without mussing a single hair on his head; and Bruce Willis was always in the wrong place at the wrong time. But, these legends of action all paled in significance to the great one whose sacred star I planned to kneel before and pay homage. It was Arnie's star that I sought.

Arnold Schwarzenegger has probably the most astounding Hollywood story of them all. The Austrian-born star began lifting weights at the age of 15 and won his first Mr Universe title at the age of 20. He then won Mr Olympia, the biggest prize in the sport, a record seven times. He went on to become a mega star in Hollywood, the governor of California and he married Maria Shriver, the niece of the late US President, John F. Kennedy.

If you were to imagine what acting and speaking skills a person would need to not only become a star, but also a politician governing what was then the world's eighth biggest economy, this behemoth would hardly seem to epitomise any such qualities.

That said, his most famous role, and the one most attuned to his natural vocal prowess, was that of a machine sent back in time in John Cameron's *Terminator 2*. Anyone who thought Arnie had found his acting niche as a gun-wielding jungle commander in the movie *Predator*, was blown away by his ability to embody subtle movements and to vocalise the highly complex speech of a robot in *Terminator 2*.

What made his role so interesting was that it was one of the first times that a human had been paid millions of dollars to act like a robot. If anything, mankind spends billions of dollars creating robots that act like humans in every area of life. The story that made Arnie famous portrayed a massive threat that is increasingly becoming a reality in the world of work. *Terminator 2* portrayed human investment in the increasing sophistication and integration of computing power, only to watch that system on which mankind had become completely reliant, become self-aware and ultimately hell-bent on destroying its creator.

Do you think this is fiction? Microsoft's artificial intelligence algorithm, Cortana, correctly predicted the results of 15 out 16 matches at the Brazil Soccer World Cup. Investors around the world increasingly rely on algorithms to make financial decisions involving trillions of dollars. A Hong Kong firm has just appointed an artificial intelligence tool to its board of directors and has given it equal voting rights. More alarming for us is a study completed by Oxford University, which estimates that in the next two decades, 48% of all current jobs in the world could be replaced by machines.[27]

Our mechanical future

From the time of the Luddites – textile artisans in England who destroyed the first cotton-spinning machines in protest against the start of the Industrial Revolution in the 1800s – mankind has watched technology take over ever more sophisticated jobs. At the same time, the Industrial Revolution also created significantly more jobs.

According to *Measuring Worth*, real earnings in Britain hardly changed between the beginning of the 1300 and 1850. They have since tripled.[28] Industrialisation did not eliminate the need for human workers; it instead created employment opportunities that were sufficient to cater to the needs of the 20th century's exploding population.

---

[27]   *The future of employment: How susceptible are jobs to computerisation?*, Carl Benedikt Frey and Michael A. Osborne, September 17, 2013 http://www.oxfordmartin.ox.ac.uk/downloads/academic/The_Future_of_Employment.pdf (accessed 7/10/2014)

[28]   http://www.measuringworth.com/graphs/graph_1.php (accessed 7/10/2014)

What's more, the work of visual statistician Hans Rosling suggests that in some countries, life expectancy increased from an average of 40 years in 1810 to well over 85 by 2014.[29] It also created a massive increase in real wealth from an average per capita income of $400 to over $40 000 for the same period.

So, if the Industrial Revolution created significantly longer lives, more jobs and greater real wealth for us all, what do we have to fear? It appears that the new wave of technology advancement could be having the opposite effect.

Instead of rising incomes, real wages in America have remained largely stagnant over the past decade. Unemployment in most developed economies is staying the same or increasing, the World Bank says.

Are machines no longer tools that make human beings more productive? Are they now becoming producers, thinkers and designers that could replace us all together? The Oxford study developed a very interesting infographic showing which occupations in the USA were most at risk of being replaced, and how many people were employed in those positions. You can see the infographic by scanning the QR code at the end of this chapter. It shows how careers in various services, sales, manufacturing and office support – on which hundreds of millions of American employees now rely – have a very strong possibility of disappearing in the next 10–20 years. It also shows how careers in healthcare, community service, arts and media demonstrate the least probability. Things are moving so quickly as technology enjoys accelerating returns and grows in power at an exponential rate. This theory

---

[29] http://www.gapminder.org/videos/200-years-that-changed-the-world-bbc/#.VDB0xeNdWkA

was developed by Ray Kurzweil, who Bill Gates calls "the best person I know at predicting the future of artificial intelligence". Google has just hired Kurzweil as the head of its Artificial Intelligence division. The company has just been on a spending spree to acquire many innovative starts-ups in cognitive computing, artificial intelligence and human robotics.

The First Generation Computer, built by IBM and Harvard in 1944, weighed five tons, incorporated 500 miles of wire and was 8ft tall and 51ft long. It had a 50ft rotating shaft running its length, turned by a five-horsepower electric motor. Nowadays, there is more computing power in a nanobot, which is small enough to be inserted into your bloodstream.

This makes for difficult reading if you are in a career that, according to the Oxford study, has even a medium chance of becoming completely replaced by technology over the next two decades. But, the reality is that these forces have been shaping markets for years, and it is our responsibility to respond to them. We need to be ahead of the curve because, if we just conform to the status quo, we could find ourselves becoming obsolete, replaced by machines that have been modelled to perform the job that we have been doing for years – but at a fraction of the time and cost.

Preparing for the future

So, how do we prepare ourselves for the coming of the machines? The authors of the Oxford University study also provided very interesting insights into what they called "bottlenecks to mechanisation". Understanding the things that people struggle to mechanise is surely our best defence against robots. The three main weapons identified in the study include social intelligence; creative ability and finger dexterity. Social intelligence includes skills such as social perceptiveness, negotiation, the ability to influence people to change, and the capability to care. Creative ability speaks to one's ability to come up with innovative solutions to problems, develop inspired ideas and create unique pieces of art that appeal to our humanity.

It becomes very clear then how engaging in a Breakaway helps people to develop the skills that are required to thrive in a century dominated by technological innovation. Such experiences involve stepping out of our comfort zones to explore opportunities outside of the conventional grooves.

In a study conducted in 2012 by William Maddux and Adam Galinsky in conjunction with the Northwestern's Kellogg School, 200 students were asked to solve the famous Duncker candle problem – an experiment to measure creativity.[30] They found that 60% of the students who had lived abroad could complete the task, while only 40% of people who had not, got the exercise correct. Most Interestingly, time spent just traveling showed very little correlation with increased creativity. Only when people became active catalysts in creating, taking themselves out of their comfort zones and challenging themselves in a travel experience, did it pay dividends.

It is hard to know if we are in a war against the machines, or whether we need to greet with excitement what Ray Kurzweil calls "the time when artificial intelligence overtakes our own". It is interesting that just as easily as something can be copied by a machine, it can be hacked by humans. For years, the royalties of musicians, film-makers

---

[30] *Cultural Borders and Mental Barriers: The Relationship Between Living Abroad and Creativity*, William W. Maddux, PhD, INSEAD; Adam D. Galinsky, PhD, Kellogg School of Management at Northwestern University; *Journal of Personality and Social Psychology*, Vol. 96, No. 5.

and software designers have been eroded by the pirating of copyrighted material. But, this ability to steal is not nearly as significant as what is becoming the open source revolution. People are developing all manner of technology that is being given away free to the world.

Although we may worry about technology taking away jobs that we need in order to earn money, that very same technology could also take away the need for money entirely. 3D-printing, combined with open source software, could completely transform the global economy. Companies in China are 3D-printing houses for less than $5 000. A band recently took to the stage playing 3D-printed instruments created by industrial designer Olaf Diegel. Will we soon be able to complete a 3D-scan of our bodies and then model open source fashion designs on our virtual avatar that we can then download and print?

Scientists have been using 3D-printing to create synthetic tissues for some time. Creating complex organs has always been the challenge, yet already this year Professor Melissa Little and her team from Queensland University were able to grow a tiny kidney in a laboratory dish.[31] A human kidney normally costs in the region of $40 000.

Technology is also facilitating sharing and a free-trade economy. Now people can rent their homes, cars and almost any replaceable product for a fraction of the cost, while challenging many established industries. AirBnB has people in the hotel industry worried. Relay-Rides, the peer-to-peer car-sharing service, together with Uber, are getting motor companies to buy into the resource-sharing revolution. Kickstarter is allowing people to take on the role of banks as they help entrepreneurs raise money for their new ventures. Those small investors

---

[31] http://statements.qld.gov.au/Statement/2014/5/23/plan-to-print-3d-kidney-tissue-using-qld-expertise (accessed 25/04/2014)

helped Allerta Inc. raise nearly $10.3 million for a watch that links to users' smart phones via Bluetooth. Its funding goal was a mere $100 000.

Decentralisation has become another significant gift of technology. Many people are used to relying on key institutions for what they need. Traditionally, that would include being hooked up to a grid to receive water, electricity and phone services. The companies that provided these services had significant power over our livelihoods. Now people can survive off the grid completely. Solar power is practically halving in cost each year, making it cheaper for people to remove themselves from the electricity grid. Dean Kamen, the man best known as creator of the Segway transporter, has created the Slingshot, a machine that can produce about 250 gallons of water each day – enough to sustain 100 people – using sea or swamp water and no more energy than is required by a standard hand-held hairdryer.

Like much of the future, we have no idea where technology will take us, but that does not mean that we should not be clear about the opportunities and threats that face our vocations. The key focus of a Breakaway is discovering a career that will be fulfilling, but also sustainable in the way that you offer value in the marketplace.

However, machines will never be able to model imagination, inspiration, a sense of meaning and creative problem-solving abilities – all of which we, as humans, can access. If we are indeed in a fight against the machines, our curiosity and lack of "programmability" is our best defence. That does not mean that there are not huge gains to made by partnering with technology, but use it for innovation rather than job security.

As a result, a Breakaway should be used to discover new ways in which to create and use the products that we need. Working towards a career that could be replaced by a machine is as redundant as working hard to save money for something that technology could offer for free in the future.

THE BUTTERFLY

As my body submerged into the icy water, I felt my muscles contract, pushing the air out of my lungs. I let out a whoop as the crystal-clear elixir of the forest pool revitalised my being. I was alone as I swam naked and showered under waterfalls in the heart of the Ecuadorian highlands. The sensation of being bare in such a pure landscape allowed a truly special communion with nature.

After I put my clothes back on, I started walking down the river creek. Then I felt its presence. Something was out there, screaming at my intuition, like the call of a howler monkey. Without hesitation, I began to run. Jumping from rock to rock, swinging off tree roots and gliding through crevices in massive boulders, I navigated the gorge as quickly as I could.

I paced harder and faster, instinctively feeling that I was partaking in an ancient ritual; a timeless moment in which predator and prey engage in nature's most powerful dance.

It was gaining on me. Its presence swelled up inside of me, a wave of primal fear and raw anticipation. A sixth sense, lying dormant in my body for millennia, roared to life and allowed me to traverse the maze of natural obstacles with the elegance of a gazelle.

Suddenly, like a flash of an ancient memory, I knew my pursuer. I could smell the stink of rotten meat on his breath; the taste of blood that drove him to chase, and me to flee. The hint of flesh that would mean the difference between fulfilment and hunger, between life and death!

He was no stranger. We had known each other for millennia. I had just forgotten him, his legacy buried in my psyche, thanks to the conveniences, safeties and certainties of our age.

Now in the depths of the forest, he had risen out of the primordial chasm of my subconscious to remind me of my true nature. He brought me back to a time when our greatest freedom was to run wild in the wilderness. He was my ancestor.

As we danced, I felt the sensation of rock under foot, the chill of a cold breeze as it caught the beads of sweat on my pulsating arms, the cry of the toucan bird, the rushing of a river stream. It was pure presence.

I don't know how long we ran together, but when I came to the end of the creek, he was gone. I stood alone on the river bed, my heart beating like a drum. We would meet again soon, for I knew that I could not deny my true nature nor forget my past. We would run again.

Parkour is a nature-based form of what is commonly known as urban running. It was developed by French soldiers who observed the training rituals of African tribal warriors, but it has been practiced by man ever since we first consciously used nature as an environment in which to play and train. Besides the exertion of running, jumping and lifting, Parkour develops foresight, encourages strategic planning and builds confidence. More importantly, it gives us the ability to fulfill ourselves in the present by engaging in ancient practices that were critical to our survival in the past.

Archetypes are rituals, symbols and feelings that are stored in our genetic make-up. Any time our ancestors discovered or practised anything valued, the practice became a part of who we are and what it means to be human. Nowadays, we are driven to be more innovative and, as a result, we constantly look to create the future. By doing this, we neglect our past. To feel complete, we need to run through the forest like an Inca warrior, set sail for far-off lands as Columbus did, and cry out from the summit like a San scout. Breakaways give us the opportunity to recommune with ancient archetypes that are the key to our lifelong happiness.

I spent several weeks in the Ecuadorian highlands and cloud forests. As in the Galapagos, I experienced truly archetypal forms of nature and engaged in the most primal of rituals. The rainforests were so lush, fresh and green that I felt revitalised just walking the jungle trails. The thick foliage created long tunnel-like passages, taking me deeper into the bosom of the wilderness. Just when I felt that the jungle was going to swallow me whole, I would emerge into a beautiful forest glade or at a waterfall creek, feeling completely reborn.

I observed plants that I had never seen before, with colours so rich and natural designs so fantastic that I could be forgiven for thinking that I was in a scene from *Avatar*. Although Ecuador was foreign to me, the environment felt familiar, as if I were retracing my ancestors' footsteps.

Many psychologists claim that for people from urban environments, the catharsis felt from being in nature is actually the overcoming of a form of homesickness. Humans have lived in cities for only several hundred years – literally the blink of an eye when compared to the age of Earth.

For millions of years, the natural world has been our home: a wilderness where we felt a deep connection to everything else. Humans share 90% of the genetic code of every other living organism on the planet, yet in the cities and through the rise of technology, we have become cut off from so many of the living things to which we are intrinsically linked.

In the forest, the smell of the decomposing groundcover reminded me of the cyclical nature of life. The sight of long vines cascading down from the tree canopy appealed to my most primal sense of the forest as my playground. As I walked, the feeling of the hard earth below my feet grounded me. The world is a chaotic place, but walking through the jungle brought me back to my most fundamental sense of existence, I was a part of Earth and of the beautiful systems that I saw all around me. Returning to the wilderness is a Breakaway from the urban shackles. It also offers one the opportunity to connect to lost family members on the most fundamental of levels.

Arriving at a 30ft waterfall with Emma in tow, the only way to continue on our journey was to jump, or to navigate a rickety ladder that looked even more hazardous than throwing ourselves into the river. The wooden steps were rotting and seemed that they would give way at any moment. Every archetypal drive told me to launch myself into the depths of the waterfall. Tons of water were cascading off the rock face and thundering into the abyss below.

Emma, overcome by the fear of the jump, decided to take her chances on the ladder. When she was safe at the bottom, she could take the photographs that would demonstrate my leap of faith. So, it was agreed that she would go down first, but only after I had tested the integrity of the ladder.

So, I went up and down what I considered to be a very dodgy, but ultimately safe, ladder. I felt that if she went down slowly and held on to the metal railing on the side, she would be fine. Like a scene from a movie in which a firefighter helps an old granny out of a burning building, step by agonising step she eventually made her way to the bottom. When she had recovered from the trauma and readied the camera, I prepared to jump.

The moment was petrifying. Although I knew it was safe to jump from this waterfall, as I had spoken to locals in the area, I had no one to follow. On this particular day, I would be the first. It brought me back to the idea of the first ancestor who would have been standing on this very spot for the first time. I reflected on what he or she went through. Having previously treated the waterfall as something that should be feared, that person had suddenly decided to fling themselves off the edge for no other reason than to embrace a sense of adventure.

Rocking back and forth with my feet perched precariously close to the edge, I slowly summoned up the courage to jump. Emma would lead the count. *One ... two ... Wait! Are you going to jump on the count of three, or after?"* she screamed, clearly more nervous about the jump than I was. Having engaged in the typical dramatic alignment for the photograph that gave some respite from the reality of a commitment from which I could not return, we agreed that she would shoot on the count of three. My heart was thumping.

One ... two ... three! A little run-up and off I went, accelerating through the air. The time between jumping and hitting the water must have been a few seconds, but it felt like an adrenaline-filled eternity as I braced myself for landing, shaping my body like an arrow.

Splash! Suddenly I was underwater and the deafening sound of the waterfall became all-consuming as my world went black. Breaching the surface with relief, the intensity of the moment receded, allowing me to regain my breath and to confirm that I was uninjured. With a thumbs-up from the photographer, I felt alive as I made my way out of the cold mountain water.

The jungle trail extended for long distances, and we had the opportunity to cross an archetypal rickety bridge and even swing from a rope that made us feel like Tarzan. Finally, we made our way to a butterfly sanctuary on the edge of the small village in which we were staying. Butterflies of all shapes and sizes turned the skyline into a magical dance of iridescent colour.

At the sanctuary, we were able to view all stages of the butterfly's life cycle: from cocooning to hatching and flying off into the ether. Their little chambers for metamorphosis looked like coloured earrings hanging from the trees. We could not escape the reality of death as deceased bodies of all varieties scattered the floor like confetti. The butterflies, which would live for a few weeks, provided a stark reminder of the nature of life itself.

My career dies

One of the main catalysts in my decision to engage in my latest Breakaway was that for some unknown reason, I had completely lost my passion for my work. I could not understand it and, more importantly, it felt very personal, as if there was something wrong with me. What made my loss of inspiration, energy and direction so baffling was the effort that I had put into creating Elixir. I thought it was my ultimate vocation and the perfect business. I had been thorough when trying to create a venture that, to the best of my current awareness, was the optimal balance of all the things that fulfilled me. The combination of nature, personal development and travel were as fulfilling as I could hope for. After four years, the business was finally gaining significant traction, my product portfolio was developing a track record, and I could count some of South Africa's biggest companies and schools as my clients. I was living my dream!

But, as if out of the blue, my enthusiasm for my work and business dissipated. It was if one month I had been completely engaged in my work, then the next, I was lost, confused and depressed.

Asked why people want to go on sabbaticals, the most common response is burn-out, stress, a desire to travel or the need for change. But, what is the cause of the stress or the desire for change? What causes people to suddenly become bored by a job that used to fulfill them on every level? How do those people who were fuelled by their careers suddenly wake up desiring to pack up their stuff and go away? If people had perspective on what they were experiencing, they might go on Breakaways for the right reasons.

The cycles of life

Nature clearly shows us that life is dominated by cycles. The ones with which we are familiar are the seasons, the tides, the moon and the migration of animals. My experiences in the Galapagos reminded me that often we have to adapt to change that comes from external forces beyond our control. In a modernised world, this includes recession, actions by the government, decisions by our parents or even cultural shifts. We have spent the last few chapters exploring the influence of changes in education and technology. We constantly need to be researching in order to ensure that the product we want to offer, or the vocation we want to develop, meets the needs of the marketplace and responds to these trends.

Although aware that change comes from within us, too, while I was in Ecuador I began to understand that there is a fundamental cycle of which many of us are unaware. During our lives, we expect to go through a cycle of ageing, over which we have no control. Our bodies change and, as a result, our values and emotions start to shift. Without this change, there would be no development and we would stay infants, unable to fully embody the cutting-edge of human evolution.

What went wrong?

When we reflect on our careers, we often think that we are in control of our choices. We can choose which company to work for, in which department to position ourselves, and which opportunities to pursue. Of course, the powers-that-be will always have some influence on our progress and, to some extent, over how quickly we move up the ladder.

As an entrepreneur, I had more control over my career than most people enjoy. I could choose what products to develop for which markets. Obviously, in order to be viable, the products had to add value and meet a need, but I could still decide what I wanted to do. This freedom allowed me to work with large multinationals; smaller, dynamic businesses; schools filled with vibrant students; and also entrepreneurs. Besides the wilderness, I engaged a multitude of tools, including music, dance, creative problem-solving and a host of other fun modalities. I exercised choice.

The profound conclusion I reached in the forests of Ecuador was that I had some degree of control over most things in my business, except for one thing: how I felt about it. On the verge of my Break-away, work that used to sate the very core of my being began to have less meaning. The vision that used to inspire me no longer motivated me.

While working in the personal development field, I had been given many tools to help myself and my clients to cultivate the emotional resources required to pursue audacious goals. Before this vocational "breakdown", I had created a vision that had a host of exciting objectives towards which I worked. Many of them I met, others were still to be realised. Connected to this was a financial plan that I had created for myself, and a really good routine involving friends, spiritual practices, exercise and relaxation. So, I thought that my loss of inspiration was my fault. If I had created what I thought was this perfect business, the problem had to be with me. Perhaps I had a bad attitude, a negative outlook, or just a lack of gratitude for everything in my life. So, I made gratitude lists, tried to remind myself why I had developed the business in the first place, and did all manner of meditations, visualisations and affirmations to try to reclaim my inspiration. It never returned.

What happened? Were my expectations completely wrong? Had I hyped up my ambitions so much that I had set up my career for a complete anticlimax? Why was I suddenly taking no interest in what I thought were my deepest passions? Was there something wrong with me?

Many successful entrepreneurs and professionals have experienced these emotions and grappled with these questions during their careers. But, what causes us to realise that we are feeling lost and uncomfortable, and to suddenly take a journey inward? What prompts us to question our purpose, explore our values and dissect what is making us feel this way?

Many people have completely abandoned their endeavours and ventured out into the unknown to try to discover that "thing" that feels right. It is very common for people to continue in established careers or businesses only in the interests of "never quitting", or out of a fear of risking what they may have created over the years. Some people are so heavily burdened by the financial responsibility of bonds and school fees that they would never risk stepping out into the unknown, while others sacrifice their true emotions for the sake of not going against their word, or for the expectations of society and family.

A lack of integrity in one's self usually leads to burn-out, stress and even depression. People quit their jobs, sell their businesses or turn to other forms of escapism, such as medication, to avoid the realities of their lives.

Renewal

I watched as the butterfly, which had begun the cocooning process as a brown hairy caterpillar weeks before, emerged as a beautiful green example of nature's transformative power. It would take some time for the butterfly to gather itself before suddenly taking flight for the first time.

That moment in Ecuador took me back to an amazing quote that my mentor, Mark Dodsworth, kept on his desk, but that I had never really been able to apply to my own life and career development with any resonance:

> *"What the caterpillar calls the end of the world, the master calls the butterfly!"* – Richard Bach[32]

When I was going through that really confusing and painful time in which I questioned Elixir and my life in general, I had not actually lost the passion for what I was doing. I was simply going through a renewal.

The key question to ask yourself is: Are you satisfied with what you have achieved and the way things are? For me, the answer was: "No". I

---

[32] *Illusions: The Adventures of a Reluctant Messiah*, Richard Bach, Mass Market Paperback, 1989

finally understood that to be open to new creative opportunities, there had to be a detachment from past endeavours. As painful as it was, it allowed me to Breakaway fully.

This was taken one step further by an amazing model that I learned in coaching school. Created by Frederic M. Hudson and Pamela D. McLean, this model appears in the book *LifeLaunch: A Passionate Guide to the Rest of Your Life*.

The idea that we go through a cyclical renewal is not an easy one to fathom, as we often consider our lives to be a linear progression in which we grow older. Hudson suggests that within each life stage, there is a cycle of renewal similar to that of a butterfly.

For the baby boomer generation – people born just after World War II – it was considered normal to keep one's job for life. That is why many of our parents are what we call professionals, such as lawyers and doctors, who have had only one career during their lifetimes. Generation Y – people born in the mid 80s – are expected to change careers four to five times in their lifetime. Who knows how often Generation Z – people born after the new millennium – will change their careers.

But, what prompts us to change direction? Is it just about moving into new careers that are invented by other people – responding to an ever-expanding range of opportunities that become available out there? Or, are we responding to some cycle of renewal happening within us – the urge that gets us to step out of the normal confines of our thinking into something new, innovative or extraordinary?

Any new career developed by someone else is ultimately their own response to some cycle of renewal within themselves. If we were not motivated to detach from old ways of doing things, the world would not even come close to reflecting the diversity that we now take for granted.

Hudson's model describes the various "realities" of our life at certain stages of our endeavours. It describes how, despite all logic and rational explanations, we suddenly feel negative and pessimistic about our greatest accomplishments, only to step into a completely new stage of optimistic energy and creative abandon.

Figure 1: The Renewal Cycle

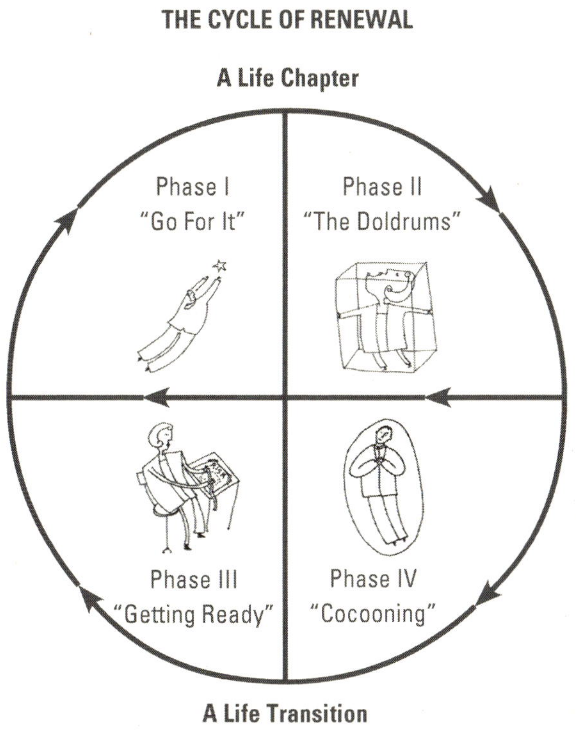

THE CYCLE OF RENEWAL

A Life Chapter

Phase I "Go For It"

Phase II "The Doldrums"

Phase III "Getting Ready"

Phase IV "Cocooning"

A Life Transition

The renewal cycle was developed through the observation of key stages of a cycle with which we are all cosmically in tune. The model is extremely important to our understanding of why we would want to Breakaway and what we can expect from our experiences. This helps us

Breakaway in the right way and avoid unnecessarily sabotaging careers that may still be ideal, but that simply need some creative renewal.

The first phase is called "Go for it" and speaks to those stages of an endeavour in which we feel active, busy and committed to our objective. We experience a level of optimism, energy and clarity of purpose in what we need to do. This is where we experience so many pleasurable emotions and are inherently good at following through on the logical plans we have developed in order to get us to this stage. We find ourselves able to proactively tackle the challenges and opportunities that come our way with a firm resolve.

Make way for the new

As I became uninspired by my Red Zebra work, I was naturally withdrawing to make way for what would become Elixir. I was so engrossed in the development and implementation of the new business plan that it almost consumed my every waking moment. I was waking up before dawn, working my day job at Red Zebra, and going to bed after midnight as I put in place my exciting vision. When I left my job and focused on Elixir full time, my life returned to normal and the business fulfilled me for a number of years.

The second phase is where things start to get interesting. Suddenly we have to deal with different emotions. According to Hudson, when we are in the "Doldrums", our emotions could be dominated by confusion, sadness or sheer dismay. Like animals who suddenly feel the urge to migrate to better feeding grounds, we too feel a restlessness and dissatisfaction that calls for new growth.

Having detached from the pleasurable emotions that would have kept us following the same routine and world view, we now have to embark on a new journey to fulfilment. Our energy levels drop, and we turn from team players into pessimistic loners who are resistant to following through on new ideas. This stage can be hugely challenging for people if they do not understand why it is happening, or the ultimate purpose of growth. I had been working on the Elixir business for four years and clarity, direction and inspiration were being replaced with confusion. I felt lost and uninspired.

Cocooning

Just as a storm often forces us underground, the escape from the doldrums requires us to go into a stage of "cocooning", when we turn inward to explore a new set of emerging values and emotions. After a period of upheaval and pain, we find ourselves healing as we deconstruct the experiences of the past and reconstruct ourselves in our new form.

As we prepare for the next stage, we find ourselves tapping into our resilience and the core spiritual purpose that underpins everything that we do.

I know that had I not cocooned and found some respite from the doldrums, I would never have had the physical or mental resolve to survive my next stage of renewal. That was when I decided that I needed to Breakaway in order to explore new opportunities that sat completely outside the realms of Elixir.

Once we have completed our cocooning phase, we enter the "Getting Ready" stage of new purpose, in which we feel driven, creative, free and naively optimistic about the future. It is as if our very inner child is at work while we search out new opportunities and network with people.

I began to make mind maps; travel books found a home on the coffee table and surf guides sat comfortably next to the toilet – the ultimate throne of exploration. During that time I had the brainwave that would become the *Breakaway* book. It would be an awesome sabbatical project that would tell the narrative of my year of exploration while being able to offer something tangible to people who would follow in my footsteps. Little did I know that it would become a transformation of my original Elixir business and not the radical change that I had feared while I was in the doldrums. I would eventually go back to coaching with even greater resolve, thanks to the higher purpose that I discovered through my Breakaway.

Rebirth

My cocoon was starting to break and I was hatching. It was now time for me to cast myself out into the unknown. But I knew that the cycle of renewal would continue, and I would possibly find myself witnessing the disintegration of my former self once again. Armed with this important knowledge, I could greet this metamorphosis with fascination and curiosity as I observed a new way of being emerge. It could have meant a new career, a new business or just a revitalisation of my old self with renewed creative vigour and a deeper understanding of ways to add value by using my skills.

Your turn

Reflect on where you currently sit right now in terms of the cycle of renewal. Consider how you feel right now about your career, and what you need in terms of a Breakaway.

KIDNAPPED

EL SALVADOR

I don't quite know why I agreed to go back to the home of a complete stranger. Perhaps it was the invitation of a well-dressed man with an American accent to experience a unique carnival celebration in the small village in which he had grown up. It may also have been because I had arrived at the border much later than anticipated, and El Salvador has a reputation for being one of the most dangerous countries in Central America.

Standing alone at the deserted border post, the promise of a home-cooked meal, a family's hospitality and a unique cultural experience seemed like a dream come true. A few hours later, while I was being driven into the barren countryside, I feared that I would not be enjoying any of those things. The sneaking suspicion that I had been kidnapped crawled into my consciousness like a spider.

We tend to think of criminals as dirty, uneducated and covered in tattoos. But, such figures are just smokescreens for the real operators, master salesmen who make you feel at ease while they take everything from under your nose. "Andy Garcia" was a good-looking guy with gelled hair, a smart shirt and a Samsonite suitcase. I was the one who looked out of place as I crossed the border with a big surfboard bag and "Gringo" (Spanish for foreigner) written all over my forehead. It was the photograph of his children and his girlfriend that had put me at ease. He had asked me questions about my trip, my family and more specifically, my ability to fund such an experience.

We jumped into the taxi that would take us to the pick-up point where we would meet his cousin. I could not help being taken aback by this family man's interest in the local El Salvadorian ladies, especially the younger ones. While we sped towards the town, he practically howled out of his window at the passing girls.

The taxi dropped us off at a Burger King, where Andy proceeded to chat up a girl who could not have been older than 16. Finally, after almost half an hour his cousin, Louis, arrived. He was a short man with a large moustache, and he sported a Stetson hat with the integrity of a real cowboy. Louis immediately informed us that our home-cooked meal would be courtesy of Burger King, and it seemed that Andy relished the opportunity to buy the 16-year-old girl dinner. The conversation over our Whoppers was limited, to say the least. At that point, I wondered whether I would have been better off taking my chances at the border post. Something didn't quite fit. They did not seem like family men.

In his car, I was startled when Louis revealed a massive hand gun, which he assured me was for my own protection. For a population of six million, there are about 500 000 guns in El Salvador. The 16-year-old girl had not climbed into the car and thanks to my limited Spanish, I had been unable to ascertain why she was not joining us. I feared I had perhaps missed my opportunity to escape a rounding-up of strangers by a group of kidnappers.

During the hour-long drive into the middle of nowhere, things became even stranger. Andy explained that Louis had 30 children. Due to a decade-long civil war that had ravaged the country in the 80s, the ratio of woman to men had increased to a startling 20:1. Apparently, Louis's grandfather, who was the most powerful landowner in the region, had more than 50 children. Thankfully, the bizarre story shifted my perception of these men from potential kidnappers to national heroes who spread the fruit of their loins to avert a gender disaster. Even though the country's gender ratio has since been restored, I still got the feeling that these guys had trouble controlling the old reflexes.

While driving through the countryside, Louis pointed out the huge expanse of his family's land. At the farmhouse, I was greeted by a very simple dwelling. In the living room, I was shown a wall that sported a multitude of photos of his children. Cursing that my camera had recently broken, I tried to burn into my memory what appeared to be a family tree going back 20 generations.

That evening, we were to attend the town carnival in San Alejo. The celebration lasted from the 6-18 January, and there were significant activities organised for every night of festivities. I simply assumed that the local disco would be playing the same Latin American pop songs that had been abusing my ear drums for the past six months, but I was greeted by a full street party boasting more than six stages that would rival the production quality in any major capital. Christmas and New Year would definitely have been important events in a town with such a strong Catholic culture, so it was a mystery to me how these communities found the money and energy to sustain so much partying.

I discovered that the El Salvadorian economy does not have many significant assets. Since European fabric makers stopped using indigo to create dyes in the 17th century, the country has been looking for something to give it a competitive advantage. The answer came in the form of immigration. Almost a sixth of the population now slaves away in the United States, sending relatively large amounts of money back to their relatives at home who, in turn, indulge in month-long festivals.

Walking through the streets with Louis was like being part of a gangster's entourage. Not only was he flanked by two mean-looking Latinos, but we had to stop repeatedly so that people could pay their respects. Whether that was because he had dropped his trousers, or he had aided them in more traditional ways, eluded me.

During my travels, I had met a guy from Australia who had been looking to set up a surf hostel in El Salvador. He had abandoned his mission after discovering that most landowners had to pay extortion money to one of the two rival gangs who are responsible for most of the crime in El Salvador. As a large landowner who did no such thing, Louis could not have held on to his assets without getting his hands dirty. Despite his boyish face and casual demeanour, this little man was obviously not someone with whom you messed.

The lack of men had had another impact on El Salvador. Although the boy band is a staple of commercial music around the world, in El Salvador it was as if the Backstreet Boys had just released their first single. On every stage were groups of camp-looking boys throwing out dance routines to the delirious crowds.

I had an amazing night with Louis and his crew. Although there were thousands of people in attendance, I did not see any other foreigners. To enjoy such a unique experience was a privilege. Hopefully the carnival of San Alejo won't appear in the *Lonely Planet* for some time to come.

Latin America suffers from an incorrect perception of crime. Any travel guide for South and Central America would strongly advise against trusting a stranger in the manner I did. Mind you, if one was on the London Underground or at JFK Airport, it is highly unlikely that the average person would go home with a stranger, either. Have we completely lost our ability to trust helpful strangers? How can we have real travel experiences without doing so?

If one looks at the travel routes around the world, one will find that everyone follows similar routes. This is due in part to the stringing together of popular travel experiences over time. With a constant flow of tourists to a particular place, more companies begin to offer cheaper commercial tours, better transport, global travel facilities, and various levels of accommodation. What is not often discussed is that people tend to follow the same routes because they are afraid of going somewhere that could pose a risk to their safety.

Any time there is an incident in a foreign country, travel books are obligated to list it for the benefit of their readers. Reading about just one of these incidents can steer people away from a place. Yet, most of us happily get into cars, play dangerous sports, eat badly and even smoke. At times, we take these risks out of necessity; at others, the perceived pleasure outweighs the risks; and sometimes we are just in denial or plain ignorant. The level of risk is based on the quality of the reward.

Peter Grey, a research professor of psychology at Boston College, is an expert on play. I was fortunate enough to interview him and discuss his book, *Free to Learn*[33]. According to Grey: "The ability to play is one of humanity's most valuable traits. It is responsible for our success as a species, but it is in significant decline." He believes that from an evolutionary perspective, play is the most important factor that gives young mammals the skills they need to survive and to develop into adulthood.

---

[33] *Free to Learn*, Peter Grey, Basic Books, 2013

Grey makes a very important distinction, which forms the basis for this chapter. Play is defined as an activity that is self-controlled and self-directed. The only people who control anything are those who are engaged in the organic, undefined process. What we call games, or sports, are nothing more than a diluted construct of this vital need. Grey believes that "play is now an artificial environment that caters more to the fears of parents than to the exploratory capability of the young". Travel routes depict a similar attitude of complete risk aversion.

Grey also cites several studies that show how children in the developed world are given less time to play. He also notes a correlation between a decline in play and an increase in depression, student suicide and a decreased sense of people feeling in control of their lives. Play is the very thing that gives young people an appreciation for the fact that they can control their lives by testing and pushing the boundaries that govern their environment.

We have never been in greater need of the qualities that play provides. The Industrial Revolution gave us clear and conventional career paths with an emphasis on developing specific skills that allowed us to fit into a clear set of predictable opportunities. We are now in the age defined by Ray Kurzweil's *Law of Accelerating Returns*[34], in which the exponential increase in technology, innovation and disruptive changes has made life anything but predictable. People now need to be socially flexible, adaptable and able to work in teams.

Most changes can also be noted in what employers seek out as the most important qualities in their potential staff. The National Associa-

---

[34] *The Singularity Is Near: When Humans Transcend Biology*, Ray Kurzweil; Penguin, 2005

tion of Colleges and Employers in America, a non-profit group that links college career placement offices with employers, ran a survey asking hiring managers what skills they prioritised when hiring college graduates.[35] Here, in order of importance, are the 10 skills employers say they seek:

1. An ability to work in a team.
2. An ability to make decisions and solve problems.
3. An ability to plan, organise and prioritise work.
4. An ability to verbally communicate with people inside and outside of an organisation.
5. An ability to obtain and process information.
6. An ability to analyse quantitative data.
7. Technical knowledge related to the job.
8. Proficiency with computer software programs.
9. An ability to create and/or edit written reports.
10. An ability to sell and to influence others.

Swedish Technology incubator Hyper Island, in collaboration with Edelman, the world's largest public relations company with links to several influential organisations across the globe, conducted a unique study called *Tomorrow's Most Wanted*.[36] The results of the study showed that more than 500 business leaders suggested that 78% of the most important qualities were related to someone's personality. These included flexibility, creativity and drive. About 53% percent of the qualities were related to cultural alignment and the ability to make

---

[35] http://www.naceweb.org/about-us/press/skills-qualities-employers-want.aspx (accessed 5/10/2014)

[36] https://www.hyperisland.com/community/news/hyper-island-executive-study (accessed 5/10/2014)

decisions based on values shared with their organisation, while 39% were related to skill sets.

Grey also cites research conducted with rats that were denied the opportunity to play, but allowed to engage in every other social norm. The study found that rats that were denied the ability to play were socially crippled. They froze with fear when faced with demanding and unexpected circumstances and they retreated to corners without exploring the situation at hand. They also reacted to their peers with unwarranted aggression, suggesting that they were unable to decipher the social signals that play helps to develop.

It seems that play is probably the most important education that a person can have. However, it has to be organic, self-directed and self-controlled, so there will always be some risk involved. My experience in El Salvador was truly magical. But, in order to experience the core of any country's culture and to remove ourselves from the beaten track, we have to be prepared to take risks.

Of course, we can never be sure what the outcome may be, but the one thing that I have learned from travelling is that no matter where you are in the world, there are several vital currencies in life that are required for success: intuition, presence and the ability to go with the flow. Careers are no different.

I am by no means suggesting that people should be fool-hardy when travelling. Making an unprepared leap into the void can be as dangerous to a full-life experience as never taking risks at all. But, Breakaways are a time when we have to treat the world as our play-ground, with no agenda other than true exploration, and we have to engage with life in unexpected ways. This has to be done without completely negating the risks or denying the realities of life. In its essence, play is about exploring a reality in which the level of risk is completely unknown. Our experience of navigating this risk is what teaches us the skills to not only survive the jungle of the 21st century, but also to thrive in it.

Your turn – Time out

It is really exciting to build a period of time into your Breakaway in which you have no idea what you are going to do or where you are going to end up. It is also an archetypal value that supports our need for true exploration. It is play in the truest sense as you will have to engage with people and experiences that sit outside your comfort zone, and it will test your most important survival skills.

🌐 ACTION

Consider the following:

1. Where in the world would you like to play with no agenda or plan?
2. How many play windows would you like to have in your Breakaway?
3. Define a rough time limit to those play times.

21ST CENTURY NOMAD

The art of hitch-hiking is something you learn very quickly on Australia's Great Ocean Road. In one of the safest and most law-abiding countries in the world, it gave this traveller, who had just grown used to manoeuvring the chaotic roads of South America, the impression that Australia was a backpacker's paradise.

The lack of serious crime of any nature in Australia has resulted in the media scrambling for any newsworthy headlines. Cats caught up trees are often serious business, and while I was in the country, I actually saw a bill on primetime news, pronouncing: "Scientists learn that puberty causes emotional problems and behavioural changes."

That said, during the 90s, several hitch-hikers were murdered by notorious serial killer Ivan Milat. The story exploded in the media like an atomic bomb. More than a decade later, I would discover that the Milat murders had left most residents weary of hitching in general.

These are the few hitch-hiking basics I learned: never wear sunglasses. Eyes are the windows to the soul, so even though you have nothing to hide, you don't want to look like an escaped convict.

Secondly, putting on the "poor me" face of an abandoned orphan does little to illicit the sympathies of a potential lift. Most people who do stop, view doing so as an opportunity to meet people, learn about different cultures and to help a lone traveller. No driver wants to entertain someone who looks like they need a psychiatrist more than a lift. Finally, I discovered that a beaming smile does not do you any favours either. No one wants to be hijacked in their own car by annoying salesmen or door-to-door purveyors of fast-food religions. The key, I learned, was to exude a confidence that said to the driver that they might be lucky enough to spend time with me.

As I prepared for my backpacking adventure in Melbourne, Victoria, which is the gateway to the Great Ocean Road, I was filled with a nervous excitement. I had a tent, a few basic camping supplies and my surfboard. While packing, I had picked up a glass of water that I had laid on a table only hours earlier. After taking a sip, I felt something strange crawling around inside my throat. I gagged and spat out a spider the size of a poker chip. There could not have been a more appropriate welcome to Australia.

The real sting, however, would not come from the host of creepy-crawlies for which the country is famous, but from its currency, the Australian dollar. In 2013, the economy was booming and being a net exporter, there was significant demand for the host of commodities that were essentially the bedrock of China's growth.

After Central America, arguably one of the cheapest places in the world to visit, I was shocked and questioned how I would afford a whole month of travel in arguably one of most expensive countries in the world. The answer would forever change my world view, what I saw as the true essence of travel, and the way in which I wanted to design my life.

I arrived in Apollo Bay, a small holiday village that is the gateway to the legendary Great Ocean Road. I had a whole week ahead of me to explore literally hundreds of kilometres of pristine coastline. "Aus", as it is affectionately known, is unbelievably beautiful. Out of all the amazing roads winding across this massive island, this route was said to be the best. The road was built by soldiers, who after returning from World War I, were given free plots of land along the Victoria coastline as thanks for their service to their country.

Besides keeping their able bodies and shell-shocked minds busy, the soldiers built the road as a tribute to their friends who had not made it home. The route winds out of Apollo Bay, round the Otway Peninsula, past the Twelve Apostles – one of the most majestic natural spectacles – and finishes in the small town of Port Campbell.

The Great Ocean Walk is an eight-day epic that navigates a 104km route that takes one even closer to the majestic coastline than the road. This would have been impossible with my surfboard. As the bus from Melbourne pulled away, leaving me standing at the bus stop at Apollo Bay, luggage in hand, I had no idea where to go next.

I was still not sure how I was going to get around. Hiring a car was just too expensive. There was a possibility of catching a more affordable, but highly infrequent, bus that would take me the entire way, and I was still not completely convinced of the receptiveness of Australians to hitch-hikers. When I told people I was considering hitching, they regaled me with stories of Ivan Milat, as if the murders had happened yesterday. Not one to be scared off, I started walking up the road while trying to decide whether I was going to be brave enough to put my thumb out.

Standing on the corner of the street at the edge of town, an empty road lay before me. I was going to go for it. As I put my hand up for the first time and before I could fully extend my thumb, a car stopped.

Shocked at how easy it was, I thanked the American couple with the vigour of someone who had just been saved from a stranded island. Once I had calmed down and they had bundled me into the back, we were off.

In another great example of the synchronicity that Breakaway's provide, the woman, Suzy, was contemplating becoming a life coach and was delighted to be able to pick my brain for the next few hours. In fact, they were so interested in my journey that I got the feeling that it might be difficult to lose my first lift. Luckily, they were a delightful couple and we went on a fantastic walk together before they dropped me at the Johanna Beach free camping spot.

If there is any means of travel that embraces the Breakaway spirit, it is hitch-hiking. Driven at first by financial necessity and then by sheer exhilaration, it became my modus operandi of exploration and discovery. Instead of rented accommodation, individual transport and organised travel, I no longer had any clue where I would pitch my tent for the night, how I would get there, or who I would meet along the way.

Besides being the essence of a Breakaway, hitch-hiking is also a fantastic metaphor for the choices we face when exploring and choosing a career. I could have easily driven the whole way with the couple I met on the first day. They were driving through to Port Campbell, stopping at all the attractions I wanted to see. The lure of definite transport with people I liked was strong. Ideally, though, I wanted the experience to be about meeting as many people as I could and embracing the full spectrum of Australian culture. In our careers, we are often quick to sabotage the opportunity for diversity of experience in the name of convenience, safety and becoming "successful" as quickly as possible.

Over the course of the week, I travelled with more than 17 different parties. Some I rode with for only half an hour, and others became my travel friends for a couple of days. In each instance, I was given a rare window into people's journeys; how they lived their lives, built their careers and contributed towards the cultures they represented in their communities.

On some occasions, I had to wait in the middle of nowhere for a lift for several hours. I remember standing in the beating sun at a traffic light where literally hundreds of people stopped, but they did everything in their power to avoid making eye contact with me. As the time ticked away, I felt even more orphaned by society. The primal alarm bells start ringing with fears of abandonment, survival and acceptance. Then, in a moment of generosity, someone picked me up and took me on a new adventure.

The spectrum of different people I met on my journey was quite extraordinary. I learned from the personal assistant to an Australian minister what it was like to prepare for an election and to manage a constituency. I was also picked up by the Male Bag Ride, a prostate cancer fundraising campaign that involved men riding little red bikes from Perth to Melbourne to raise awareness of the disease. The organisers gave me a unique insight into what it was like to co-ordinate a project of that scale. I even had the chance to talk to David Parkin, one of the riders who was an AFL (Australian Rules Football) hall-of-famer. In Victoria, that could be likened to speaking to the prime minister.

I met a road worker, railway maintainer, tour guide, accountant, and asset manager. Over the course of the week, I had essentially managed to interview 17 different people representing 17 different vocations. Breakaways create a massive opportunity to learn about other careers and opportunities that exist in other countries.

I had been on my Breakaway for almost a year, but I met more people while hitch-hiking during that week than I had met in months travelling and staying in traditional backpacker establishments. I believe this is owing to a trend that is unfortunately undermining the traveller's spirit and the essence of backpacking: the accessibility of iPads and smart phones.

In days gone by, a refuge was a traditional place of safety used by people on pilgrimages. They were humble spaces, but what they lacked in facilities, they more than made up for in atmosphere. People, all walking on the same route but on different journeys, would sit by candlelight and share stories of their experiences on the road.

Any pilgrims arriving at the refuge late in the night would be welcomed by the sight of people silhouetted by burning fires and the sound of warm, welcoming laughter. The refuge would eventually become what we now know as the backpackers' establishment. Gone are the days of humble furnishings. Some accommodation rivals that of boutique hotels.

Irrespective of comfort, backpackers' were different from hotels because the culture was based on refuge, participation, sharing and fellowship. Unfortunately, this culture is shifting. The communal spaces that would once upon a time have had the whole establishment sitting around a table talking, now feel more akin to internet cafés. People sit in isolation with their heads down, keeping up with a world from which they are ultimately trying to Breakaway.

Through all manner of tools, such as Skype and Facebook, people have the opportunity to stay in touch with friends and family back home, while using the internet to plan their trips. Although useful, these benefits should not detract from the opportunity to fully detach from our lives and the opportunity to experience a real journey.

Technology as an escape and a distraction is the story of many people's lives. We rely so heavily on the internet that many young people can't differentiate between virtual escapism and reality. It is vital that anyone wanting to fully Breakaway unplugs, opens themselves up and removes themselves from their comforts.

I met Nathan at the Johanna Beach camp site. I had left my surfboard in Apollo Bay for fear of not being able to hitch-hike with it, so he was kind enough to lend me his after seeing me sitting on the beach staring longingly at the perfect waves. Our campsite did not have electricity, let alone wi-fi or mobile phone reception, so we shared some amazing stories under the stars and agreed that we would take a walk together the next day.

While walking, Nathan told me a very valuable story that would come to define my experience on the Great Ocean Road. He was reading the book, *Walden*, by Henry Theroux. Written in the 1800s in the US, the book is described as a personal declaration of independence, social experimentation, a voyage of spiritual discovery, satire, and a manual for self-reliance. One story that Nathan shared with me from the book described how Theroux had agreed to meet his friend in Fitchburg, a small town 30 miles away.

His friend had encouraged Theroux to join him on the relatively new railway that could transport them to the town in less than 30 minutes. Fitchburg was an eight-hour walk away, and Theroux was adamant that he would rather walk. His friend was amazed that he had not seen the value in paying for a new service that would get him there in a fraction of the time.

Theroux explained that even though the actual train would take 30 minutes, his friend would have to work for more than eight hours in order to make the fare. While he went on a fantastic walk through the woods, his friend would be toiling away to afford the opportunity to ride on a busy, noisy train that would eventually get him there more slowly and require more intensive work than walking would. In every respect, Theroux would have the better journey.

Nathan was a trained doctor and his reading of *Walden* was part of his exploration of his fundamental needs. It was an opportunity to clear out the clutter and to get to the essence of what he knew he wanted from life. Human beings have a very interesting way of approaching fulfilment. This approach shifts the results we get from our lives. The following two stereotypes illustrate this dynamic well:

Wall Street is often called the home of capitalism and consumer-driven society. Without doubt, the extreme poster boy of this community is Jordan Belfourt, known best as the *Wolf of Wall Street*. Wall Street's primary focus is profit, money, power and material possessions. It is often assumed that people in this industry focus on what they would like to "**have**" – a billion dollars, a Ferrari, a mansion in Greenwich, a yacht and their own nightclub.

In response to what they desire, these people clarify what it is that they need to "do" in order to "have" what they want. This may include studying an MBA part time, accumulating significant student debt, working 16-hour days in order to climb the corporate ladder, starting a multinational company, or travelling the world building a business over 50–60 years. As a result of what they "**do**", they will have a certain way of "**being**".

Consider your assumptions about what the "**being**" of such a person would entail. What feelings is such a person looking to fulfill by doing all of these things? Do they want to feel significant? To be accepted by their community? Or is there a need for growth?

A monk's primary focus is attaining or "**being**" in a state of enlightenment and presence – a spiritual place dominated by freedom from suffering, desire and the obsession with earthly possessions. To maintain this "being", they "do" meditation and maintain their silence. They become aware of their ambitions so that they can understand their ultimate objectives and overcome any hook that suggests that they need to "**do**" or "**have**" something in order to "**be**" a certain way. As a result of what these monks "do", they "**have**" certain things.

One of the most famous monks of all time was Romana Maharshi who, at the age of 16, retreated to a cave in the holy mountain of Arunachala, in India. There, he remained in spiritual contemplation for the rest of his life. Living there in that simple dwelling, eating and drinking only the most basic meals, he guided a community who gathered around him and joined in his spiritual practices.

These two types show the vast differences in how our approaches can meet our core emotional needs. The latter spends most of his time focusing on being in the present, while the former is committed to the future, with less regard for his present being. Although these are two extreme examples, neither approach is right or wrong. They only differ in their consequences.

Life is all about choice, and we have the ability to find an approach across the spectrum that works for us. The challenge is that when we live in a certain community for too long, the dominant values and life approaches become the status quo and the benchmark of success.

To feel accepted by a community at a drinks party in the Hamptons, New York, you would need to hold all of the attributes that define success within that community. If you shared with the other guests that your company had recently listed on the stock exchange, you would probably be congratulated and invited back again. But, chances are, you would receive only looks of astonishment if you shared your ambition to live in a cave, free from material possessions, for the next 10 years.

The purpose of an effective Breakaway is to explore cultures that practice different approaches to finding a balance between **having, doing** and **being**. Breakaways also allow us to explore different communities, to appreciate their values and to understand what fulfills us most. These choices will impact where we live, what companies we join, what communities and societies we support, and how we define success.

* * *

Nathan took me back to Apollo Bay so I could pick up my surf board. We enjoyed a couple of waves together and then he left me once again on the side of the road to face the unknown. I thoroughly enjoyed meeting him, and I trusted that along the spectrum, he would find the right balance that worked for him. Little did I know that the next day, I would meet the person who was living the essence of "being" that most appealed to me, but to the extreme.

I had been standing on the side of the road for ages, anxiously waiting to get a lift to a surf break down the coast. I saw a young-looking guy drive past in a van. He looked me in the eye, appeared to contemplate for a second, and then carried on around the corner without stopping. His van had surf racks on top of it, so I was disheartened to see him drive on.

The knowledge that some really good waves were breaking out there without me to ride them was adding to my impatience. Suddenly, 10 minutes later, the man in the van returned. His name was Andrew. When he asked me where I was going, I replied that I had nowhere else to go but to find some good waves. He had been doing the exact same thing for seven years.

Some of the happiest moments of my life have been spent surfing waves. For the past seven years, Andrew had lived his life in such a way that it would optimise his ability to enjoy what we both so enjoyed: surfing. He was a professionally trained chef, and the amount of time he worked was meticulously calculated to maximise the time he spent in the ocean. As a result, he lived in a campervan that allowed him to sleep next to the sea. Aboard his little surf mobile, he had a full kitchen, bed and a lounge that he opened out on to the area in which he parked – usually a beach. Coupled with this, he had internet, movies and anything else that he may need to distract his wave-crazy mind when his body was too exhausted to surf any longer

For three days, Andrew and I patrolled the Great Ocean Road looking for waves. Together, we travelled hundreds of kilometres and surfed excellent breaks. While I sat in his van, listening to the adventures of a man who was already well travelled but still intended to circumnavigate the whole of Australia's coastline – a length of 35 000 km – I was both challenged and inspired by his way of living.

Did I have the courage to commit my whole life to surfing? What were my non-negotiables – the things that I felt that I had to have or do? A nice car, a big house, a comfortable retirement or a good education for my children? Where these non-negotiables my own, or rules that had been passed down to me by my parents or by society at large?

Sitting around the campfire with Andrew, I wanted to dig a little deeper, to try to find the cracks beneath this perfect veneer. Every part of me wanted to buy a van and live life the way he did, but I knew there was something that I was not seeing. Was he running away from something? Was he lonely? Was his way of living unbalanced or extreme?

He acknowledged that his lifestyle did not allow for the development of deep friendships. Having met hundreds of people on the road, his mission often meant frequent goodbyes, many of which were sad. The lifestyle did not allow for a woman in his life, unless he was lucky enough to meet a kindred spirit who shared his nomadic approach and was happy to regularly use public toilets.

His career as a chef would never develop further than that of a temporary worker. He acknowledged that he might get bored with this way of living, but at that time, he was not worried because he had committed to the things that he loved. He always had the option to specialise in his career, or to shift the balance and surf less.

When Andrew left me at the station in Torquay, the spiritual home of Australian surfing, I had mixed emotions. Torquay's legendary break is Bells Beach, and the fact that I did not even surf it indicated how much I had veered off the beaten track. Watching his battered old camper van disappear on the horizon, I felt really grateful to have met this 21st century nomad.

Irrespective of whether I would end up following in Andrew's footsteps, I learned something very valuable on the Great Ocean Road of Australia: the whole backpacking experience reinforced that the journey is always more important than the destination. The people I met and the generosity of spirit I experienced were far richer than the places I ultimately wanted to visit.

I was challenged to examine this destination of "success" that I was chasing. To Breakaway, we often need to experience truly unique and unusual ways of living, so that across this amazing and vast spectrum that we call life, we can find our own balance.

The rise of the amateur

As we discussed in the previous chapter, the 20th century was undoubtedly the hey-day of the corporation, as well as the professional. The Industrial Revolution made the sciences, engineering and financial institutions the true powerhouses of the global economy. To be accepted and viewed as an agent of change in an industry, or in the economy in general, one had to complete certifications, climb the corporate ladder and subscribe to formal systems that were used to regulate the professional world.

If you wanted to be taken seriously, you had to become a professional. This movement gave rise to the conventional routes that were regarded as the easiest paths to acceptance in the professional world. Clear grooves were cut in the education system. Once people had negotiated these paths and "arrived", they were regarded as the source of all innovation and expertise within those specific areas.

Amateurs have traditionally been thought of as people with an interest in, or a passion for, a specific activity – but who have careers in completely unrelated areas of expertise. Given the choice of how to spend their time, they would undoubtedly engage in their passions instead of being at work. The motivator for their professional careers is largely money.

The term "amateurs" implies that the passion that is not the primary career would not provide a level of income required to survive. As a result, such people are not prepared to take the risk of abandoning their work to become professionals in the fields of their amateur passions.

Alternatively, such people are very happy with the time distribution between their professional work and their leisure time. With no high-level certifications, rankings or positions within influential organisations or associations, amateurs are often regarded as inferior to professionals.

The professional-amateur blur

The Pro Am Revolution is a study completed by Charles Leadbeater, an expert at the Demos Institute in the United Kingdom.[37] The pro-am

---

[37]   *The Pro-Am Revolution*, Charles Leadbeater, 2014 http://www.demos.co.uk/publications/proameconomy (accessed 9/10/2014)

economy explains how the line that divides professionals and amateurs is blurring significantly. This is happening for a number of reasons. Firstly, people do not subscribe to the same traditional boundaries of work and leisure that they used to.

During the baby boomer generation, one generally worked from 9am to 5pm, Monday to Friday. What one did outside of that time was called "leisure". Now people are taking their amateur leisure activities more seriously and upgrading them to professional levels. By engaging with their passions, they are developing high-level skills and expertise and becoming part of communities of influential amateurs who create powerful clusters of expertise. As a result they develop one, or sometimes two, shadow careers as "pro-ams".

This development of skill and clusters of expertise have made pro-ams a very powerful source of innovation. They are more likely to consume the products relevant to their industry with a greater degree of intensity than amateurs or public consumers. Because pro-ams develop powerful communities that are bound by a shared collective passion for an area of expertise, there is a far greater cross-pollination of ideas and development of practical solutions than in industry-leading companies.

Many pro-am innovations are huge disruptors and can completely change the way that an industry is run. The whole notion of finished-product innovations coming from boffins tucked away in company laboratories and then passed down to consumers, is over. Realising the power and influence of pro-ams, large companies are now opening up their products to scrutiny, refinement and in-use improvement by groups of dedicated innovators that exist outside of the company: the pro-ams.

Andrew was a very passionate surfer who may go professional one day, thanks to the number of hours he has surfed. But, he was not only a passionate amateur surfer, he was obsessed with everything related to nomadic living. He took the art very seriously, and I witnessed things like his mobile surfboard repair station and his roof travel compartments that he had developed and installed himself. Andrew was a pro-am traveller and I could be seeing some of his inventions ending in a camping store very soon. He could potentially add these skills to his existing profession as a chef to create a cluster of vocations that all could provide income, meaning and fulfilment.

Your turn – Developing your Breakaway Launchpad

How much will your Breakaway cost? Everyone feels the need to answer this question before they embark on a journey of this scale. Ultimately, we want to know that we can afford such an endeavour, but usually we are trying to establish whether there will be a return on our investment. The reality, however, is that the value of true exploration can never be clarified, so no return on investment can be calculated.

In the same spirit, if I asked you how much your life will cost, you would probably say that it was impossible to work that out. You don't know how long your life will be. Secondly, you can live your life on a spectrum, from basic to ultimate luxury, but you really don't know where you are going to be in 30 years' time and what opportunities you may encounter along the way.

That said, you can establish what major things, like houses, cars, school education and holidays, will cost you in order to provide a rough idea of how to focus your financial strategy. Again, we return to the Breakaway paradox of embracing our ability to plan and control our lives in the face of complete powerlessness.

We still need to put a peg in the ground. For this reason, I would like to introduce a rough schedule and financial plan for your Breakaway that can be developed on completion of this book. Most importantly, it allows you to open your mind to developing income from your vocational clusters on your Breakaway and beyond.

Let's consider the various aspects of your Breakaway in terms of cost centres, and how you can go about making them more efficient.

Long-term vocational journey

These are your most meaningful vocational options. You have established that you have no experience in them, so you are not going to invest in education, internships or any resources related to them, until you have taken them through the research cascade. As a result, the only cost related to exploring a long-term vocational journey is the money required to engage in observational days, or work experience weeks.

Short-term vocational projects

As we have discussed, the focus is more on finances. That is not to say that you won't be passionate about various projects which could ultimately make for a very strong, sustainable pro-am vocation. That said, you'll need to take cognisance of the income potential from a short-term project, and the related costs going forward. For example, I am also a DJ. It has always brought me in extra income, yet I have had to invest in buying the equipment that is a prerequisite for being a professional in that area. I could use my pro-am skills as a DJ to create income on my Breakaway.

Specific travel costs

There is no escaping the cost of flights and of gaining access to specific activities on your Breakaway. You may want to fly to Brazil to attend a world music festival or a prestigious training programme. These costs are very easy to establish and incorporate into your plan.

This does not have to stop you from identifying creative ways to nullify these costs. People with creativity and networking skills can find ways to develop mutually beneficial partnerships. The person who is attending the festival in Brazil could arrange a volunteering contract in exchange for a ticket, food and accommodation. They could be paid to get what they needed in the first place: work experience related to a vocational option.

General travel and living costs

Books such as the *Rough Guide* contain up-to-date information on the daily budgets required in different countries. They even offer different budgetary levels: basic, middle and luxury. When you engage in your time of play, these budgets will be very important because you will have no idea where you will be going or what you will be doing.

You also need to be very clear on the basic living costs incurred when you are at home. You may be doing work experience or observational days in your own city. Incorporate these weekly or monthly costs into your budget. You may also receive a stipend – a nominal fee paid to interns or apprentices – so be sure to include that in your income, too.

Fixed costs

You may be in a position where no matter where you are, you have to pay certain costs, such as a bond, school fees or a life insurance policy.

Extra costs

Related to each place you'll visit, there are going to be things like visas, innoculations, medical insurance and special equipment that need to be purchased or hired.

Example of a monthly planner and budget

Month	Country and Breakaway experience	Specific cost of activity or flight	General living cost or travel budget	Extra or fixed cost	Total cost	Income from stipend or short-term vocation	Surplus/ deficit
Jan							
Feb							
Mar							
Apr							
May							
June							
July							
Aug							
Sept							
Oct							
Nov							
Dec							
					Total	Deficit or surplus	

The Breakaway Compass

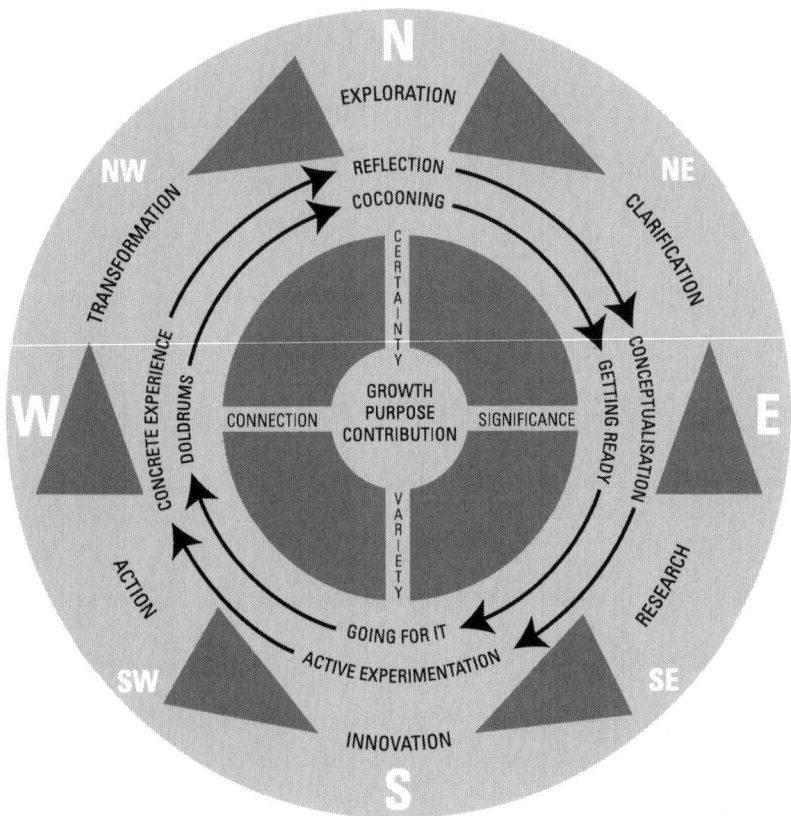

Source: J. Behrmann

Having completed your Breakaway Launchpad and having designed your ultimate Breakaway you are now stepping out into the unknown.

The truth of individual vocation development is that it often requires courage, integrity and creative problem-solving, rather than just following the herd in an unconscious way.

When it comes to exploring and discovering your unique vocation, no one can tell you where that destination will be. Even the best maps in the world struggle to provide an exact picture of the terrain. In this case, the terrain speaks of your unique state of mind, beliefs, life experiences, inspirations and mission, which no parent, school or company can predict or map out for you.

As a result, you need to be fully aware of how things are constantly changing so that you can adjust your Breakaway plan. If you just blindly follow through with a Breakaway schedule, you will miss the essence of what these experiences are all about – navigating and responding effectively to change.

The whole objective of the compass is to ensure that you make conscious decisions while revelling in the wilderness of your Breakaway. So many things have the potential to unsettle you as you set off into the unknown. By conducting a Breakaway, you are giving yourself the gift of choice by expanding your range of opportunity. This extra choice can bring further complexity.

Furthermore, in order to afford this window of exploration, you have potentially put yourself at financial risk and have perhaps sacrificed everything that you have left behind. This may be a position in a company, or your family, friends or a significant other. The temptation will always be to run away from the emotional upheaval that comes from heading outside of your comfort zone.

The difference between impulsive actions and conscious decisions is usually the time dedicated to exploring the choice, the degree of self-awareness, and the research on which a person has based the decision – along with the level of emotional intelligence that informs the quality of the decision-making.

There is nothing worse than the regret that comes from feeling that you have sabotaged yourself out of an opportunity for growth, or that you have let a great opportunity go by because you became fearful, overwhelmed or lost in the complexity of change.

The reality is that we never really know with 100% certainty whether we are on the right path. All we can know is that our decisions are made based on our best self-awareness and emotional resilience.

So let's introduce the layers of the compass and how you can apply them to specific situations on your Breakaway.

Layer 1: Emotional Needs

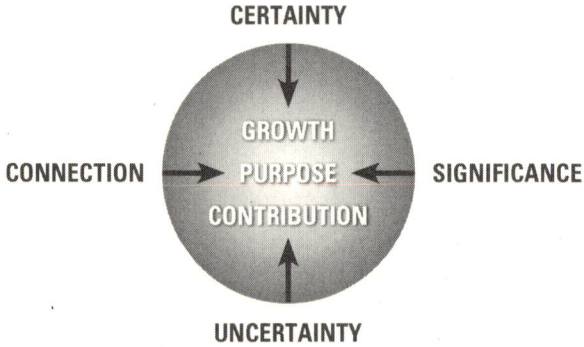

We are constantly trying to find fulfilment in our lives. Breakaways are intended to help us discover what fulfills us and to then to help us base our life decisions on our most important values as they change or emerge. To understand fulfilment, which is about the ability to satisfy a value, one has to understand need.

We all have needs. If we don't eat, sleep or breathe, our physical bodies will break down and we will die. My experiences in the Cradle of Humankind reminded me of the fact that at one point, the pinnacle of human fulfilment was to survive another day on a small pocket of land in Africa. Now, some human beings are not fulfilled unless they feel they have achieved peace across a globalised planet.

No matter how primitive or sophisticated the set of values, they can all be distilled down to the achievement of core needs that are expressed and felt in us, through emotions.

These emotions are the catalysts for action, and they can either lead to conscious decision-making or to impulsive reactions on our Breakaways.

When it comes to your Breakaway experiences, you can use this layer in order to understand the following:

a) What emotional need or sensation am I experiencing?
b) What is contributing towards this feeling?
c) Is it just a fleeting sensation, or is there a pattern emerging?
d) Does is it require action?

This model, which I adapted from a framework by one of the godfathers of coaching, Tony Robbins, firstly helps people to understand the needs themselves, and then secondly, how to navigate the conflicts that arise.

CERTAINTY – Survival/control/routine

Many of our strongest emotions are spent repeating patterns that ensure our survival. For those of us who are lucky enough to not have to wake up wondering whether we will make it through the day, we create routines, systems and plans that give us the feeling of certainty that we have some control in an unpredictable world.

Such examples include:

• Following conventional career paths in order to feel a certain level of success.
• Travelling only to safe countries in order to feel certain of our survival.

- Going to the most popular destinations so as to feel certain that we will have a good experience.
- Feeling uncertain when leaving a career that has been a source of security.
- Feeling uncertain when we do not know what to do with our careers.
- Feeling uncertain when our bank balance drops while on a Breakaway.

VARIETY – Uncertainty/surprise/change

Moving in the exact opposite direction of certainty is our need for variety. In a world where everything is certain, routine and controlled, we grow bored, restless and our human drive for curiosity becomes irritated, like a sore that needs to be scratched.

Such examples include:

- Sabotaging ourselves out of careers that become too repetitive.
- Not planning our Breakaways in ways that allow us to feel a sense of surprise or adventure.
- Embracing the uncertainty of not knowing where each day will take us.
- Feeling the need for a change of location.
- Feeling bored in an internship and wanting more experience.

ACCEPTANCE – Community/love/connection

Families, organisations and even potential partners all have their own values, beliefs and cultures. The primal need to be accepted by our tribe was the basis of survival and, as a result, being accepted by the various communities that embrace our values is a key emotional need.

Such examples include:

- Feeling homesick on our Breakaways because we crave the love and connection to our families.
- Not feeling accepted by old friends because our values have changed and we want to do something that is different from what our peer group is doing.
- Feeling that we don't belong when returning to our communities after a Breakaway.
- Feeling that we connect with the people and the culture of a specific organisation.
- Meeting with someone special and feeling that all we need is love.

SIGNIFICANCE – Being Unique/sense of individual purpose/personal identity

Moving in the opposite direction from conforming to the values of a dominant community is our emotional need to feel unique and significant and to follow our own sense of purpose that sits outside the tribe.

Such examples include:

- Following through on our own ideas of success that are different from those of our families.
- Wanting to express our own style, which is different from that of our friends.
- Going on Breakaways that fulfill our own sense of mission and adventure.
- Finding positions in companies that make the most of our unique talents.
- Discovering what values are our own.

CONTRIBUTION

Early humans learned that if they did something for their neighbour in times of difficulty, their neighbours would more than likely return the favour. This reciprocal altruism is another classic example of our genes learning that which optimises our chances of survival, and rewarding such actions with positive emotions that fulfill us. That is why we have a need to feel that we are making a contribution to the world. Whether you see this as the fulfilment of a selfish ego with a selfless act, or whether you believe that we are waking up to the fact that we are all connected in a dynamic web of life, the reality remains: we all need to feel like we are making a contribution.

Such examples include:

- Basing our careers on that which makes us feel that we are making a contribution.
- Feeling like we are adding value in internships.
- Creating meaningful legacies for our children and for society at large.
- Coming from a place of service within our organisations.
- Feeling like our Breakaway have a purpose beyond ourselves.

Growth

Many of the most successful people in the world find that when they have achieved their ultimate visions – endeavours that have taken them years of focus, energy and sheer determination to complete – they are once again unfulfilled. It appears that no matter what level of success we achieve, we are always driven to grow in mind, body and spirit.

Such examples include:

- Feeling like we want to get more out of our Breakaway experiences.
- Wanting to set specific goals that push our Breakaway boundaries.

- Sensing a lack of growth in our current internships or careers.
- Becoming restless in a specific place.
- Wanting to take ourselves out of our comfort zones.

Layer 2: Experiential Learning Layer

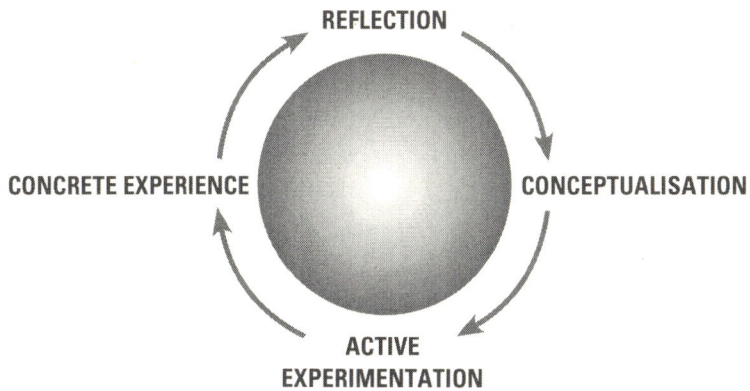

Source: *Experiential Learning: Experience as the source of learning and development*, David Kolb, Prentice Hall, 1984

If Breakaways are about learning how to be more fulfilled by meeting our needs and responding to our emotions in the most conscious way, learning becomes very important indeed!

School is very good at providing us with information to learn, but it does not pay that much attention to teaching us HOW to learn.

Is the learning process something that just happens instantaneously, out of the blue, like an "Aha!" moment, or is there a distinct, unconscious process that we go through that starts way before we have a particular insight?

The model in Layer 2 was developed by David Kolb who studied the process that people went through when learning. He found that the more people consciously went through these stages, the more powerful the learning, and the more informed their decisions tended to be.

Breakaways are valuable because they give us new experiences. If we do not fully learn from the experiences, we cannot extract the value relevant to us.

It is important that you understand this layer and how you can use this tool to maximise your learning from each experience.

Concrete Experience is about having the experience:

- Bungee jumping off a bridge, feeling the wind rush by you, the ground rushing up towards you and the adrenaline pulsing through your veins.
- Visiting a city for the first time, smelling the aromas of the streets, hearing the sounds of the market traders and feeling the atmosphere.
- Being told by your boss that you are being let go and feeling your heart pumping with anxiety as you hang on his every word.

To ensure that you make the most of a Concrete Experience, you can ask the following question:

1. Am I fully accepting of this experience as it is?
2. Have I properly committed to this experience?

Reflective Observation means that you relive the experience in your mind, assimilate the emotions, and become aware of all the thoughts running through your head. You cannot properly reflect on an experience when you are still in it:

- Watching the video of your jump, you allow the intensity of the experience to subside. You see yourself in your mind's eye flying through the air and remember what was going through your head at the time.

- Riding on the bus, you recap your highlights of the city you have just visited as memories flash by, filled with colour and vibrancy.
- Packing up your stuff from your desk, you let the words of your boss sink in and recall the thoughts that arose as you walked out of his office.

To ensure you make the most of the **Reflective Observation**, you can ask yourself the following questions:

1. During that experience, what was I aware of?
2. During that experience, what were all of my senses doing?

Abstract conceptualisation allows you to translate the reflected experience into meaning, logical theories and conclusions.

- You decide that adventure sports are your favourite vocation and that you want to potentially explore getting into the business.
- You decide that you want to live in a big, vibrant city that will fuel your need for creativity.
- Your conclude after a week of being at home that you were let go because even though you liked what you were doing, you were not actually a really good fit for that type of company.

To ensure you make the most of your ability to conceptualise abstractly, you can ask the following questions:

1. How did this experience relate to or challenge my values and beliefs?
2. What theories am I creating and what conclusions can I draw?

Active experimentation speaks to how you practice, experiment and try out new approaches based on your revised view of the world after an experience.

- Organising an internship with a bungee tour company.

- Giving yourself six months to live in your chosen city to see if your conclusions are correct.
- Having made a request with a recruitment company to explore opportunities in smaller boutique companies in your industry, begin the interview process.

To ensure you are experimenting properly, you can ask the following question:

1. What concrete experiences can I set up to test my theories?

Layer 3: Divergence and Convergence

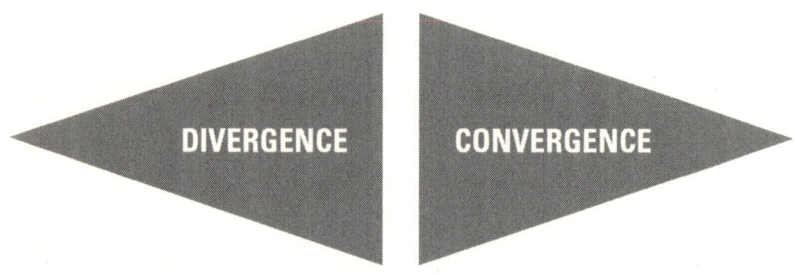

Having just reviewed the stages of learning, it should come as no surprise that the questions that we ask ourselves greatly influence the degree to which we learn and how our Breakaway unfolds.

Another key layer is the creative problem-solving fundamentals of Divergence and Convergence. We used them a great deal to design our Breakaway plan.

We diverged when we EXPLORED all of the potential vocational opportunities in the Career Constellation. We then converged when we CLARIFIED our best opportunities in the VOCATIONAL DASH-BOARD.

Again, we diverged when we RESEARCHED these opportunities as part of the RESEARCH CASCADE, with the intention that, we would then converge on a value proposition in terms of an INNOVATION that incorporates not only our vocational aspirations, but also key trends in the market, education and technology.

Finally, we diverged again as we jumped into ACTION in our Breakaway using the Breakaway launchpad, which outlines our experience in terms of a time schedule and financial plan. This Breakaway then opens us up to more divergence in terms of opportunity that we navigate using this BREAKAWAY COMPASS. Our Breakaway leads to further transformation and then ultimately a convergence on our vocation.

Any time you face a decision based on change that sits outside of your normal Breakaway plan, you always need to question whether you have diverged enough before converging on your final choice. Some examples relevant to the experiential learning model are as follows:

Concrete experience: What else could I try to do to make the quality of this experience better, or to feel that I have fully experienced everything that it has to offer?

Reflection: From how many different perspectives can I see that experience?

Abstract conceptualisation: How many different theories and alternative meanings for that experience can I create before settling on my final conclusion?

Active experimentation: What can I do to explore as many opportunities as possible before settling on the most suitable one?

Layer 4: Your Intuition

The whole objective of this practical section has been to provide you with the tools to help you design and manage your Breakaway. Having reviewed your options, you have to come back to probably the most important layer: your intuition. At  the end of the day, all you can do is make a choice and have faith that you are being guided to where you can be the most fulfilled.

THE CORE

I f there is a heaven for surfers, I am sure it is Indonesia. Clean waves peel with perfect form that even artists struggle to capture. Hundreds of breaks, many still undiscovered, are dotted along a chain of islands that create the longest national coastline in the world – 33 000 miles in total. What's more, besides being the quintessential tropical paradise with the relaxed, spiritual and welcoming people, Indonesia is un-believably cheap.

The previous month in Australia had been exhilarating, but a financial assault course, so arriving at Denpasar Airport and seeing the prices, was like releasing the constrictive top button of a tight shirt. For the cost of dinner on Bondi Beach in Sydney, I could enjoy three full meals, sleep in a comfortable, basic bungalow on the beach and rent a scooter that offered me the freedom to indulge in a feast of surf breaks. My six weeks in Indonesia were going to be the culmination of not only my Breakaway, but also a surfing dream that had enchanted me for years. To top things off, my girlfriend, Emma, whom I had not seen in months, would join me for two weeks.

My first glimpse of Uluwatu, one of Indonesia's most famous wave breaks, was like waking up from a sleep to discover that my dream was, is in fact, a reality. The swells travelled up from storms deep in the ocean and folded over the reefs on the islands, making for perfect, but risky, surfing. Every Indonesian veteran has a war story to tell about being dragged along the unforgiving, razor-sharp coral reefs.

Conquering the waves despite this reality made for an even more thrilling experience. Sitting in the line-up for the first time, I tried to control the butterflies in my stomach. My progress was cautious and I started on smaller waves and then slowly worked up to waves within my usual range. Watching the seasoned Uluwatu regulars take off on mountains of water sent a tingling cocktail of desire and fear coursing through me. As I grew in confidence and started to push my boundaries, I would commit, late in the afternoon of only my second session, to what would be a paradigm-shifting wave.

The horizon began to distort, as if the oceanic army had been called to march forth. Feeling the water level dropping as the oncoming wave consumed its surroundings and dominated the skyline, I turned and paddled. Feeling myself rising to the crest of the massive swell, I felt a chill as the wall of water blocked the comforting rays of the sun setting on the horizon. The instinctive urge to pop to my feet just as the wave was peaking sent me into a free fall down the five metre-high face of the wave. Turning to align myself with a wall of clear turquoise water, I raced down the line with awesome speed. The jagged reef glinted in the afternoon light, just a few feet below the water. Despite the danger, all thoughts disappeared in a moment of communion with the ocean.

As I sat in the water after my ride, my euphoria mixed with deep appreciation as the sun set over my new spiritual home, Indonesia.

When I woke up the next morning, frothing at the mouth with excitement at the thought of another session, I raced down to the beachfront and was greeted by another perfect day of surf. I relished the thought of enjoying this surf Mecca for another six weeks. As I ran along the beach, I slammed my pinky toe into a rock covered by sand.

After recovering from the initial pain and observing what looked to be nothing more than stubbed digit, I gave it no more thought as I paddled out into the ocean. It was only when I struggled to stand up on the first wave, resulting in a massive wipe-out, that I started to think that perhaps the injury was more serious. It turned out that this little dwarf appendage that had been of no consequence for 30 years, was actually the surfer's equivalent of Van Gogh's paint brush or Tiger Woods's putter.

X-rays revealed no break, but even after rest and anti-inflammatories, I could not surf properly. Despite a good deal of mothering from my girlfriend, she was dealing with a love-sick puppy who was facing the heartbreaking reality that his Indonesian surf fantasy had been brought to a grinding halt by a pinky toe.

A Breakaway brings alive the essence of the journey. Unexpected detours become the most surprising discoveries. Experiences that initially seem like problems ultimately bring one into contact with people who express such kindness and generosity that it transforms one's perception of humanity. What initially feels like a disaster goes on to provide the missing link in our development.

With my girlfriend back in the United Kingdom and my toe still a painful reminder of my inability to surf, I felt seriously depressed, as if I had been robbed of the surf dream I had been building towards for years. Out of nowhere, I decided to do Vipassana, an ancient meditation technique that was developed outside of India.

The essence of any Breakaway should be a voyage of self-discovery. When we feel lost, it is easy to consider travel as a way to rediscover ourselves. People spend significant amounts of time, energy and money scouring the Earth, looking for answers or a new direction.

Often people travel to escape, ignore or hide from realities at home. No matter how long they travel, or how many places they visit, they will come back to their home country and fall into their old, familiar patterns. Irrespective of how much they searched for a new beginning "out there", they will keep returning to the same inner place from which they tried to Breakaway.

Compare your conscious mind to the crust of the Earth. Mountains, valleys, oceans and great rivers all comprise the playground that we explore on our journey.

As awesome as some of the great peaks and canyons of the Earth may be, they pale in comparison to the depth and mysteries that lie below the surface: a world so foreign that the furthest man has been into the Earth's crust is a mere 3.9km of more than 6 000km – not even 0.1% of the full depth.

Western Deep Levels on the West Rand, South Africa, is the deepest mine shaft in the world. It exists not to mine for a greater understanding of life's origins and the mysteries that still exist, but for gold.

Like deep space exploration, the business case for spending trillions of dollars to plough into the Earth without any clear return on investment has meant that the core remains an unknown world that we take for granted. We continue our existence on the surface, oblivious to the fact that what ultimately shapes our lives is bubbling below the surface.

However, the awesome power of nature reminds us of one of life's ultimate truths: impermanence. Under the Earth's crust, huge electromagnetic forces cause tectonic plates to collide with an awesome power that is diluted only by time. A fast-forward replay of the Earth's formation would reveal that the planet is far from static and that nature is not being shaped on the surface, but from forces below that are beyond our comprehension.

If the conscious mind is the crust of the Earth, the unconscious mind is the massive, ancient and mysterious part of our world that we do not understand. Just as the Earth can be fundamentally influenced by its core, so our unconscious mind ultimately directs our lives. To ignore the reality of what lies below opens us up to an eruption, no matter where we think we are in our lives, or how successful we may be. Such an eruption could have unprecedented implications.

If a Breakaway is about developing self-awareness, a journey into the unconscious, as difficult and as foreign as it may seem, is a critical destination.

Vipassana's primary purpose is to help people experience true wisdom and freedom from suffering. The technique involves exploring the deepest nature of our human experience and the real source of the forces that shape our lives: the unconscious mind. Like drilling through the surface of the Earth presents significant difficulties, accessing the unconscious mind in a controlled manner requires patience, persistence and the Vipassana technique, which has been refined over hundreds of years.

When I arrived at the Dhama Java Meditation Centre, just outside of Jakarta, I was excited, despite not really knowing what I was getting myself into. All I knew was that I would not be able to speak for 10 days. I thought that it was the freedom from the compulsion to speak that delivered the amazing results many of my friends had experienced. As it turned out, not speaking was only the beginning.

The retreat grounds sat atop a picturesque hill in the central highlands of Java. From the entrance, it appeared as if the whole facility had been chopped in half by a barrier that divided men and woman.

Without the distraction of the opposite sex, we would be free to go even deeper into the depths of our being.

Looking at the daily programme, which started at 4am and involved 11 hours of meditation, I started to question whether I had what it would take to complete the course. Settling in to my spartan room after handing over all writing materials, technology and any other distractions that would take me away from being completely present, I awaited the start of the first meditation.

I had wanted to do Vipassana for years, but every time I looked at the schedules in South Africa, there was never space available, or a date that aligned with my business responsibilities. While travelling, I had looked at the global website, but had never found a convenient time, nor made it a priority.

After finally resigning myself to the fact that I could not surf, I had been sitting in an internet cafe in Bali when I was suddenly decided on Vipassana. I looked on the website and there was a course starting the following week. Coincidence? I think not.

In reality, the surface level of my world was in chaos. My relationship with Emma had suddenly hit a wall of confusion and emotional distance and I was close to sabotaging it. My brain was working overtime as I tried to rationalise, control and ultimately plan my way out of the emotions that were fracturing my well-being as the end of my Breakaway approached.

The meditation hall was filled with the deep and calming sound of S.N. Goenke, the humble leader of Vipassana, who had welcomed us to the programme. The organisation is a miracle in itself. It offers free courses in centres all around the world, receives no institutional funding and has grown sustainably as a result of donations made by people who have experienced the course. Over the 10 days, we would be housed, fed wonderful meals and given access to top-class facilities.

All teachers, servers and support staff were volunteers, who gave in the name of "Dhamma" – the powerful law of nature that we would not only understand, but experience in the time to come.

The first few days involved observing the breath in its most natural form. Any time I noticed my mind wandering, I was told to respond with complete acceptance and return my focus to the most basic indicator of the state of the unconscious: the breath. My experience was like stepping out of a torrential river and sitting on the bank while watching a chaotic stream of thoughts rush by. I was a passive observer who was no longer being washed further downstream into the oblivion of his out-of-control mind.

While observing my mind for the first time, I was blown away by the chaotic and often polarised nature of my thoughts. I felt my emotions as they tried to hook me, like the rising tide of a river that sweeps one back into a maelstrom. Once again, through awareness, I observed my emotional reactions, let them go and observed the chaotic river of my conscious mind become tranquil again.

We were then instructed to focus our attention on the sensations around our nose. This included the feeling of air entering and exiting the nostrils, throbbing in the sinuses, or the slight coolness just above the lip. Like sharpening a drill that was to cut through the layers of conditioned thinking in order to experience the subtle sensations of the body, we continued to meditate for hours.

The tranquil river of my conscious mind exploded like an under-water geyser, as it scrambled for thoughts that would allow me to avoid the sensations that were being released from the underground caverns of my unconscious for the first time. Years of anger, resentment and fear rose to the surface, turning my thinking into a vortex of irrational thoughts.

Through awareness, we observed our thoughts, did not judge them and came back to the sensations in the body, where this expression of the unconscious mind was manifesting. Again, the rampant thoughts and emotions went away, along with the sensation. The river of my mind became tranquil once again.

On the fourth day, we were instructed to use focus to observe the mind and scan every part of our bodies. Like geologists use a laser to map underground for gas pockets, fractures or pressure points before excavation, we patiently moved through our bodies, observing sensations as they arose and eventually faded away.

At first, I was only aware of gross sensations, perhaps the release of some emotional wounds from my childhood. We did not interpret or analyse the sensations, only observed them with equanimity. Eventually my body came alive with sensations, as if every part of my being was tingling with vitality, life and, ultimately, change.

Suddenly I was hit with an overwhelming desire to break up with Emma. The prison of my mind exploded with crazy thoughts of leaving her, not spending time with her in London as agreed, and simply returning back to South Africa. This confused me as she was thousands of miles away and had not done anything to provoke a sudden break-up. I fought, rationalised and scrambled for some understanding of why the river of my consciousness was now a vortex. Sitting in silence in the mediation hall, tears streamed down my face as I broke up with Emma in my mind's eye. I grieved for the end of our relationship. Unable to just observe the thoughts borne of these sensations and their apparent implications, I tried to fight them. For three days, I waged battle.

Unable to take it any more I asked to see the teacher, who was allowed to engage with each of us for a maximum of five minutes, but only around our meditation techniques. Any attempt to discuss one's history, philosophy or future thoughts would be quickly dismissed. I was lost in the spectres of my thoughts and believed that because of the sheer pain that I was experiencing, my circumstances were special. I tried to enlighten myself by sharing the details of my slowly crumbling relationship. A few sentences in, the teacher asked me if I was aware of any sensation in my body. I had spent the last three days trying to avoid these tormenting thoughts, so it was with some frustration that I said "No". She invited me to go away and to try to find it.

Still grappling with the thoughts, I carried on with my meditation. A day passed and still I was trying to stay in my body, despite being overwhelmed by the compulsion to radically sever my relationship with Emma. On day nine, weary from the battle, I became aware of a sensation on the right side of my stomach, just above my pelvis. For the next few hours my focus vacillated between the feverish thoughts that had plagued me for the past three days and the feeling that I was now trying to befriend.

The sensation was completely unique to me. Suddenly it grew and grew, as if something in my stomach was contorting under huge pressure, almost like a volcano. It reached an excruciating level of intensity, until something burst in my stomach. As that happened, the thoughts of Emma immediately disappeared, as if the torment I had suffered for the past 10 days had never happened. To this day, it remains the most extraordinary physiological reaction I have ever experinced.

Overcome with emotion, I ran up to the teacher, wanting to know what it meant. Sitting in front of her with tears in my eyes, unable to contain both my relief and sheer awe, she would give me no explanation. I had clearly made Emma the subject of a much greater wound that I had been avoiding.

The next couple of days were spent in quiet contemplation. I did not have any more thoughts about Emma while I was at the centre. At a fundamental level, I finally understood the great wisdom of which people had spoken. The universal law is that of impermanence. Everything changes. Our suffering is caused by an inability to accept life as it is, and an unwillingness to confront the anger, pain and resentment of the past.

Approaching the end of the course, I started to access a new way of being. I had worked through the discombobulated nature of my chaotic self and had processed what could have been baggage that I had been carrying around for years. I experienced a completely unique feeling: for brief and fleeting moments, there was no thought, no bodily experiences or even any comprehension of time. I experienced pure consciousness, being and freedom.

Driving out of the Vipassana centre, I felt like a new person who was experiencing life with a substantially different world view. Even though I had no idea what the explosion in my stomach had been or where it had come from, I knew that I had touched on something significant. The Vipassana had given me the gift of choice to continue my relationship with Emma. I had been a prisoner of an old wound that would have sabotaged every one of my relationships moving forward. As I would discover, the rupturing was not the main event. It was only an awareness of tectonic shifts that were going to rock not only my Breakaway, but my life in general.

THE BLIND SPOT

The skipping of the Bach CD interrupted a deep hypnotic sleep that only the ocean could provide. Although I was temporarily disorientated, I soon realised that I was where I should be: in my bedroom, with my brother, an Olympic sleeper, happily passed out on the other bed across from me. Light seeping under the door suggested that my mother was still awake. Practically tech-illiterate, there was no device that escaped her reckless disregard. This would not be the first time that I had to help her find the Eject, Stop or Play button as she stared blankly at the hi-fi, as if she had been asked to decipher hiero-glyphics on a tomb.

However, at this time of night, the skipping CD took on a whole new meaning: alcohol. When I opened the door, I expected to find her standing, swaying with her eyes closed, lost in an inebriated fantasy, as if remembering a bygone era that took her away from her painful reality. One of her favourite past-times was painting. Often, standing drunk in front of a canvas, it seemed that she would almost stab with her brush, as if frantically trying to block out some tormentor from her past. Over the years, her creations had become darker as she gradually began to lose the battles against her demons.

The repeating CD became akin to jarring machine-gun fire. It signalled that I was about to run into another battle with my drunk mother. Filled with anxiety, I burst into the living room and scanned the space. It was empty, but the patio door was open, suggesting that perhaps she was outside, looking out over the sea.

As I walked around the sofa, I saw her legs sticking out from behind the other side of the coffee table. My mother lay motionless on the floor. Although the sight of her passed out was not totally unfamiliar, something seemed different. Then I saw her face was covered in blood, as if she had been assaulted. Instinctively, I spun around, looking for some indication of a robbery or a struggle with an intruder. I was a 12-year-old boy, alone in a holiday house, while my younger brother slept and my mother lay bleeding on the floor. I was terrified.

Panicked, I started shaking her, trying to scream over the still-skipping CD, but she didn't respond. I ran to the hi-fi and turned off the dreadful soundtrack to the scene of chaos and returned to her lifeless body. After a few more frantic pleas, she stirred. "Mom, who did this to you?" I asked.

Unable to make sense of her jumbled speech, I assumed that she had been attacked. The door to the patio was wide open and there was also a trail of blood leading outside. Stepping out on to the deck, the sound of the thundering ocean in the darkness, which normally brought me so much joy, had become a cloak that hid some violent aggressor who had struck my mother.

I listened for the rustling of robbers making their escape through the thick bushes beside our house, which was right on the beach. I heard nothing. The breeze slipped with hushed tones through the network of dark, scary branches that prodded at my imagination.

Then, it began to dawn on my young and fragile mind that what had happened to my mother was not the doing of some mysterious criminal. Her condition had been of her own creation, in collaboration with the usual suspect: alcohol.

Standing over her again, I screamed at her, trying to rouse her. Mothers were supposed to provide safety, security and freedom, but the last of those perceptions were crumbling before my eyes. As I looked up, I saw my brother, Jake, only eight years old, looking on with anxious curiosity as he tried to absorb what he saw. It was more of the same drunken chaos we had endured for years.

Unable to lift my mother up, my brother and I held one arm each and slowly dragged her along the passage. Her motionless body had become an even heavier emotional burden to bear. When we got to her bedroom, we placed her next to the bed and used a cloth to clean the blood off her face before trying to put her to bed. Somehow, we heaved her safely on to the mattress and tucked her in. Seeing her safe in bed brought a welcome relief. That night began a slow reversal of roles in which we, her children, would become the parents.

My mother woke up with no memory of what had happened. Our desperate pleas and graphic recounts served only to entrench her denial.

As young children with no understanding of the disease of alcoholism, we had no way to appreciate that our mother was powerless over booze and later drugs. When sober, she was the most loving mother a child could ever hope for. She was an amazing artist, decorator and sportswoman who had represented her country while at university. She still has an amazing sense of humour. But after several drinks, she would transform, saying the meanest things to me. Often I would have to physically defend myself against her onslaught.

Ultimately, my mother, like me, was powerless over alcohol and her life became unmanageable. The hereditary nature of alcoholism can be traced back generations and predicted in one's future with alarming accuracy. But, just as with most diseases, there was a "cure". Alcoholics Anonymous offered a programme which, when followed with willingness and honesty, could provide the spiritual healing required for millions of people who suffer from this problem,

After going through the programme myself, and having enjoyed the amazing Breakaway that recovery had provided, I was left feeling even more helpless as my mother floundered through the years. Usually, the addict is the last person to admit their problem. The mind creates all types of perfectly rational delusions that allow the addict to continue abusing substances, and thereby avoid the painful emotions that are the root cause of their illness.

Over time, my mother slowly began to isolate herself, stewing in the self-pity and resentment that are the hallmarks of the disease. She stopped working, entertaining, travelling and proactively socialising with her friends. Knowing full well that alcohol could take her away from the difficult emotions of her past, she became a victim of what I viewed as spiritual bankruptcy. She chose oblivion over reality.

It is not easy for me to share this story about my mother, especially since she is still alive and close to me. I wrote it for two reasons. The story is about the disease of alcoholism and not about her character or love for me, of which she has plenty. On our deepest level, we all love our parents, but that does not mean that they did not deal the most devastating of blows during our upbringing, no matter how subtle they may have been. As children, at our most malleable, we often take on the most destructive beliefs or sense of identity that can potentially have a destructive influence on our lives.

This memory sticks out as a moment from my childhood that ultimately went on to shape my life and in many ways, my career, too. It was a major trauma that had been locked away in my unconscious. Until I had understood and embraced it, it had held me prisoner.

After my parents' divorce, my father's death, and years of having to pick up my mother's emotional pieces, I became the parent and she, the child. I tried every possible means to get through to her: control, manipulation, counselling and even pleading. I was unable to accept where she was taking her life and tried everything possible to get her right.

While first trying to understand my compulsion to Breakaway on the verge of my 30s, I always cited career development, travel and a natural rite of passage as my dominant motivations. However, I had never considered that, on some level, I was trying to run away from my mother's addiction.

Over the years, I had taken responsibility for her in what had become a co-dependent and convoluted dance that was second nature to me. It was the most dominant force in my life. I, too, was in denial – powerless over my mother's disease. I did not cause it, could not cure it, and I most definitely could not control it.

When most people are ill, we treat them with compassion. Just as I had stood by helplessly while my father was dying from cancer, my mother, too, was slowly dying from a disease. I frantically screamed at her to take a medicine that I knew was readily available, but she refused it, or was unable to consume it. That would have meant confronting the true extent of her pain, resentment and shame.

I felt that she would never come right, but I kept trying to coerce her into recovery. My frantic scrambling to pick up the pieces of her breaking life floundered for years in a sea disappointment, shattered expectations and a constant longing for her to turn things round.

When I said goodbye to my mother at the airport at the start of my Breakaway, I was extremely sad. Both of her sons were out of the country, so I knew that she would be alone in Cape Town. She had not remarried and her addiction had caused her to isolate from other people. My decision to leave the country removed a huge crutch from her life, and I wondered whether she would crumble. But at the same time I felt a huge sense of relief that I would be free from the constricting influence of her addiction. I hoped that without me to lean on, she would grow to be more emotionally and socially independent.

When faced with problems, many of us feel that running away will help us to find peace. It's true that out of sight is out of mind, but we can never ultimately out-run that which is inside of us. It will follow us wherever we go, like a cloud of negative energy, ready to rain down on us at any moment. I had hoped that being in a new country would help me to avoid the mounting anger and sadness from which I was trying to escape. I also believed that I could treat issues in isolation and compartmentalise my life. But if one organ of the body is dying, it doesn't make sense to think that the body will still thrive by focusing on the other organs.

Careers can become a safe haven. The often predictable nature of our work gives us the illusion that we are still in control in our lives. The organ of my family had been atrophying for years, and although burying myself in work had taken my mind off things for a long time, my Breakaway meant that I could no longer hide behind my work to avoid my mounting emotions.

To illustrate the extent of my denial regarding my mother's influence in my life, she was hardly mentioned until the third rewrite of this book – two years and tens of thousands of words later. After I left her at the airport that day, she would go on to potentially derail not only my Breakaway, but my life in general.

Almost eight months into my trip, I was having a truly amazing time. The world was opening up to me in ways that I could never have predicted. I had been given the chance to discover myself and the world anew! Then, while I was in Guatemala, the phone rang. It was my mother. She was miserable, and floundering again in her addiction. She had just bombed out of yet another treatment process – her seventh. Although her track record suggested that she was not going to give her recovery the vigilance it required and having made the promise that I would free myself from her addiction, all of the co-dependent urges came rushing back, along with the need to play the role that had involuntarily been given to me in my youth. Could I once again drag my mother from the floor of her problems and into a safe place?

I made contact with a counsellor I had met in Cusco, Peru. He had a significant pedigree in the traditional treatment of addiction through the 12 steps, but he also worked with more alternative approaches, including amino replacement therapies and various South American medicines, such as San Pedro and ayahuasca. I knew I had to try something different and, perhaps out of desperation, my mother agreed to travel half-way across the world to complete the treatment on her own. But, I would discover, her actions reflected other intentions.

She had only been in Peru for a week when she began to bombard me with calls filled with complaints and displeasure. She had somehow managed to sabotage the whole experience and was threatening to go home unless I agreed to travel with her. Taken hostage once again by my desire to get her well, even though all of her actions suggested that she would not take responsibility for her own recovery, I agreed to travel with her. However, I had a plan.

AYAHUASCA

The small clay pot sat lightly in my hands. Even though it was only a couple of inches tall, it was an intimidating sight. The contents of the vessel were ayahuasca, one of the most ancient and powerful medicines in South American culture.

I picked it up, examined its brownish colour and noticed the way its bitter aroma exuded the essence of the Amazon, almost like a perfume. I was advised by the shaman, a traditional South American healer and intermediary between the natural and supernatural world, to drink it in one go.

Feeling like Alice staring down the rabbit hole, I was fully aware that just as my early ancestors had done, I was about to consume a paradigm-shifting substance. I drank it back and felt the earthy liquid drain into my being.

I put the cup down and came to terms with the bitter taste. I was relieved at how easily it had gone down. I stared at the rest of the people in the maloka (cabin), many whom engaged with ayahuasca almost weekly as part of a strict spiritual practice that dates back centuries. I also saw my mother, whom I had managed to coerce into coming to Colombia to drink the medicine because of its ability to provide visions of healing. She had begrudgingly accompanied me, and I prayed that not only would she open her mind to the process, but that she would receive a breakthrough. I was waiting!

Ayahuasca is an infusion of the *Banisteriopsis* vine mixed with the leaves of the genus *Psychotria*. It amazes me that such a complex synergistic potion could be discovered among more than 80 000 catalogued plant species in the Amazon rainforests. Modern minds have puzzled the origins and discovery of this great medicine, as there is no effect when only one of the two plants is consumed in isolation.

Let's put that discovery into perspective: to happen upon the right combination would mean trying more than three billion different combinations of plants available in the Amazon over an area that is five million square kilometres in size. What would possess people to consume such a nauseating substance in the first place?

Most indigenous Amazonian populations will tell you that they received instruction on how to combine ayahuasca directly from the plant spirits. For many Westerners, such an assertion is completely beyond our realm of experience. Carlos, the shaman who conducted our ceremony, was a fourth-generation medicine man and had been taking ayahuasca as often as three times a week since he was a baby. Part of his continued development included spending time alone in the jungle and receiving instruction on where to find more medicines, while building relationship with the spirits for the benefit of his community. He is one of the happiest, most loving and intelligent people I have ever met and our meeting was the tipping point in my decision to take it.

So, why consume ayahuasca? Many view it as a drug with mind- and mood-altering ingredients that pose the significant risk of taking the mind in unknown directions. At the time, I believed that I was in a healthy state of emotional intelligence and spiritual connection, so why would I risk that?

Prior to my commitment to ayahuasca, I had a conversation with a counsellor who had been helping people with a range of addictions for many years. He said he "was tired of spending months trying to weed out the roots of clients' problems through counselling when teacher plants like San Pedro and ayuhuasca could not only make people aware of the issues in a matter of hours, but heal them as well".

He went on to recount countless testimonials of people who had experienced miraculous recoveries from cancer, depression, severe back problems and a host of other issues. Ayahuasca remains one of the most effective tools for treating heroin addiction, so how could it be considered a harmful drug as opposed to a medicine? "The medicines are not just for people with problems, but should be seen by everyone as a gateway to personal spiritual development, improved health and greater self-awareness," he said.

Secondly, as I would discover, the act of taking both substances, unlike many recreational drugs, can be far from enjoyable. The medicine is seen as a mirror of the subconscious. It contains the molecule N,N-Dimethyltryptamine, DMT, which is a naturally-occurring compound that is found in all living things. It is normally released when we dream and when we die. Often, the focus of healing is seeing, in a very tangible way, facets of ourselves that we do not want to address yet need to see. Ayahuasca can also stimulate nausea, vomiting and general discomfort.

Vomiting is considered central to the cleansing process. People participating in my ceremony who frequently used both substances, spoke of purging as being a blessing and a hugely enlightening experience. Despite the side effects, there are zero recorded deaths attributed to taking ayahuasca in the correct way, under the guidance of a trained shaman.

Various people I spoke to expressed their frustration that ayahuasca is spoken of as a drug rather than as a teacher plant. They posed a different question to me: if you could go back in time and take away the freedom of spirituality, would you do so? I was quite taken aback by this. It meant weighing up what spirituality gives us and what purpose it ultimately serves.

For me, spirituality is about the quest for purpose. It is about understanding why we are here, what we are to do, and how we are to live in relation to the things around us. I see spirituality as one of our greatest gifts. It is responsible for great works of art, science, religion, poetry, and even our exploration of the stars. The purest forms of spirituality have given humanity a moral awareness that allowed us to practice forgiveness, unity and ultimately, love. It is spirituality that underpins most of our quest for a vocation. What part of spirituality was I not seeing?

Many people believe that life is merely a coincidence and that we have developed purpose to deal with the insecurity of this reality. Without a higher purpose, the sheer difficulty of life would overwhelm people who believed we were merely on Earth by accident.

Others believe that animals don't have a sense of purpose. They just survive through instinct and intuition and don't question their existence in the same way that humans do. Whether we will ever be able to prove which animals possess this capability, or why it is the sole domain of humanity, remains a mystery.

The reason for such a shift may be the intelligence of evolution, or it may be the work of a higher intelligence, call it God, Allah or Hashem. Whatever your beliefs, we cannot deny that a significant detachment has taken place which, to the best of our understanding, has taken away the permanence of the instinctual purpose that is embedded and secured in animals.

Now, a spiritual purpose is the fuel that drives our behaviour and ultimately provides fulfilment in our lives. This shift has given us the ability to reflect, imagine, conceptualise abstract concepts and ultimately, the freedom of choice to create meaning as no other species can.

Some people would prefer to remain in a state similar to that of animals – oblivious to any higher calling, without the freedom to make choices, and having to face the responsibility that comes with them. Choice brings greater complexity. When we lose the connection with our instinct, and combine it with the sheer number of choices out there, it becomes difficult to know what to do with our lives. As a result, we often just do what other people do. In other words, we conform. Many people find it far easier to escape into a myriad of distractions that dull the mind, body and spirit.

So, when the people in the maloka asked me whether I would, given the opportunity, go back and return to a time when we were not spiritual, they were actually asking me if I was ready to face up to the responsibilities of the gift of choice. This would come by expanding my mind through ayahuasca and, ultimately, my Breakaway. They were also questioning whether I believed in the spiritual realm enough to trust its wisdom which paradoxically meant that I had no choice. Were all of the experiences in my life an opportunity to build my faith in the spiritual path?

Having consumed the medicine almost an hour before, I sat next to the fire in the maloka and stared deep into the flames, observing any shift in my body. The shaman walked around the ceremony space, swinging a chain attached to a small vessel that released the rich scent of aromatic pine. Repeating melodic chants and prayers, he cleared the temple of any negative energy that would impact on our journeys. Healers were on hand to help us at a moment's notice.

Slowly the flames of the fire started to glow a much richer orange, and the blue heat at the source turned an iridescent violet. I could feel the medicine working, and we were invited to sit or lie down in a position in which we would be comfortable enough to relax without falling asleep or detracting from our ability to consciously observe our visions. I felt myself caught in limbo between being in control and fully giving myself over to the medicine. Then, like the first moment of weightlessness on a rollercoaster, I felt myself plunge.

A discombobulated haze suddenly crystallised into a vision of a giant floating mass that looked as large as a continent hovering in the sky. It came out of nowhere and then instantly dominated the heavens of my mind's eye. As soon as it emerged, I knew exactly what it was: something that I had tried to hide, gloss over or pretend that I had moved past. It was my anger – gargantuan, colossal, heavy and over-whelming.

I was used to thinking of myself as the friendly, positive and flexible Jeremy. Many of my friends would attest to a similar disposition now, yet they can all remember what I was like when I drank. The alcohol opened a chasm from which my anger would emerge, prompting fights, aggression and general chaos. I was angry, and its concealment was a defence mechanism that protected me from the painful emotions that prompted it.

Whether I admitted it or not, anger was still impacting my life; the decisions that I made; and people with whom I engaged almost 10 years into my sobriety. Anger over my father's death, my parents' divorce, my mother's addiction and so many broken expectations had been ignored with the help of increasingly sophisticated mechanisms of denial. These culminated in the giant fortress that hovered in my mind.

Even though my anger was massive, I did not fear it. Nor did I see it as a part of me. I felt that the ayahuasca was showing it to me in a way that allowed me to understand just how big and powerful it could be in my life. But, it was off in the distance and separate from me. My anger did not have to define me.

By seeing my anger, I felt like I connected to it for the first time. For years, people close to me had told me to look at my anger. It was as if their advice had gone in one ear and out the other, yet anger continued to slowly pierce my being with resentments that I kept hidden from the world. Ayahuasca helped me to face those aspects of myself that I did not want to see, but which were ultimately holding me back.

My next vision was full of amazing light and energy. A wall of bright radiance all around me created a cocoon-like sphere that held me. I could clearly see myself sitting in a cockpit. Staring out into what seemed like the universe unfolding before me, I felt a deep sense of wonder and inspiration as ancient symbols and patterns radiated out into my consciousness. I felt held by the medicine, as if in a warm embrace that comforted me after the difficult journey into my anger.

I was able to rouse myself and see that my mother was being invited into the ceremony space by Carlos, who would do a clearing. Up until then it was clear that, as in Peru, the medicine was having no effect on her. My experience had validated the reality of the medicine's effects, so when my mother, who had taken the medicine several times, experienced nothing, I started to wonder whether she was blocking the process altogether, or whether she simply could not absorb the medicine because of damage to her brain from years of alcoholism.

As I watched Carlos dance around my mother, inviting the spirits to cleanse her of her grief, I prayed that she would come right. The beautiful music created by the Andean band echoed through the ceremony space. The whole community was singing and chanting to show support for my mother on her journey. Suddenly she got up and walked out of the circle. I could see her face reflect the same stubborn reluctance that had plagued all of her previous attempts to get sober. She was fighting the process.

Suddenly my experience spiralled. A new vision emerged of me contorting in pain and grimacing from the effort of trying to bring what looked like my own little universe under control. I looked visually depleted from the battle and could see that I would be consumed by it. The ayahuasca, which had been a nurturing friend, became a tormentor from which I could not escape. I felt like it was continually hitting me with feelings of worthlessness. The shaman approached me and I told him of my pain. He said that it was not the ayahuasca that was tormenting me, but that I was torturing myself. The medicine was just mirroring what I was feeling in the depths of my being. It was clear that I was blaming myself for the failure of my mother's process, her addiction and for my inability to help her get well. He put his arm on my shoulder and told me to trust the process and let go.

After Carlos stepped away, I brought my focus back to the bamboo forest that was the backdrop to the ceremony. The large vines were swaying in the mild morning breeze, while sunbirds danced around the grasses. I closed my eyes and took in the sounds, as if they were a soothing balm to rub on my raw and battered being.

Suddenly, I felt a presence. I closed my eyes and watched as a figure emerged out of the depths of my unconscious. It was my father. He was standing before me, wearing his favourite blue cardigan. I immediately felt the comfort of his strong energy and guidance. It had been more than 10 years since he had died and I still carried regret over how I had behaved during his passing: my anger about his abandonment of me, and the sheer sadness of his plight. Most of all, I just missed his presence in my life.

He was with me. We communicated without actually saying anything. I felt everything in the core of my being. We hugged, as if to say that between us there was nothing but unconditional love. For the first time, I felt true forgiveness and a loving connection to the man with whom I shared such a complicated relationship.

Then as my father stepped away, my mother, who was lying only metres away from me asleep, came to me in another vision. She was sick, atrophied and miserable. I was overcome with grief and sadness. All of my years of struggle had been to help her become the person I believed she could be: empowered, happy, healthy and at peace with her past. Experience has taught me that you can only help people to change if they themselves want to change, yet for my mother, I could not accept where she had taken her life. To do so would mean having to face a profound sense of loss.

I really believe that my mother would never consciously choose to damage herself or those she loved. She would have to confront the sadness of the past, the shame of facing those she had harmed, and her anger towards the people who had harmed her. It was only by being honest about those situations that she could find acceptance, and ultimately the freedom of forgiveness. This I felt was a burden that she could not bear. Ultimately, though, it was her spiritual journey and I would have to accept that.

Standing over her physical body, I started to cry tears that for the first time were not out of frustration or anger, but from a sad realisation of how things really were. The tears streamed down my face as my mother lay asleep on the mattress, oblivious to the massive shift that I was making. I felt a new sense of compassion for her: the kind of compassion that one has for the sick when you are completely powerless to help them, and all you can do is comfort them on their journey.

In the early morning I would receive one final vision. In my mind's eye I saw Carlos, my shaman, meeting the San in a ceremony in the caves of the Western Cape in South Africa. The San are the creators of the trance dance – a process of hyperventilation to deep hypnotic drumming, and arguably one of the oldest known techniques of getting in touch with the spiritual realm. They have the oldest genetic code in the world. Having had so many significant visions that were so meaningful to my personal life, I was receiving inspiration to facilitate some kind of meeting of the world's great spiritual traditions in the Cradle of Humankind. Who knew what the vision really meant, where it would take me and when I would act on it, but I treated it as sacred.

My experience with ayahuasca was so significant because it gave me a tangible experience of the spirit world that I needed in order to heal. It gave me faith that I was on the right path. When the healers in the maloka asked me whether I embraced the gift of spirituality, they wanted to know if I had the courage to take responsibility for what gave my life meaning. After experiencing those visions, did I have enough faith to make them my guiding light – not only in my dealings with my family but in my future career?

In the same spirit, we have to question how we adapt to unexpected changes in our Breakaway and, ultimately, our lives. As we step out of our comfort zone and off the beaten path, we will have experiences that challenge the very essence of who we are. Often these experiences bring us back to parts of ourselves that we cannot acknowledge or that are holding us back. At other times, we will truly be in new territory and our sense of self will start to breakdown, revealing the cutting edge of our exploratory spirit.

GOING FULL CIRCLE

The wheels hit the tarmac at Cape Town Airport with a comforting ease. I had been away from my home for more than 18 months, and despite the emotional upheaval I was experiencing, I had no idea what to expect.

Table Mountain was a welcoming sight to many explorers making the dangerous voyage round the Cape of Good Hope en route to India. In much the same way, in all of the photographs that I had seen of my friends, the mountain stood like a loving uncle in the backdrop of a family portrait. It reassured me that I always had a place in the world to call my own. Its colossal presence, like the welcoming faces of my countrymen, filled me with immense happiness and pride as I walked through the airport.

It has been said that if the world was a body, Africa would no doubt be its heart. After being away for so long and having seen so many other places that could have become my home, it was clear to me that this country's energy was indeed palpable. That was the real reason that I chose to live in South Africa.

236

My mother was at the airport to greet me. Even though Cape Town is affectionately known as the Mother City, the embrace of my nearest and dearest brought back all the feelings of love and safety that had been at arm's length while I was out in the wilderness. It had been several months since my mother and I had been together in Colombia for the ayahuasca process. Tears and warm embraces flowed, together with the realisation that to return home in good health is always something for which to be grateful.

Catching up with old friends was at first a wild celebration of reunion, which became what felt like a press conference filled with a barrage of questions. Even after a couple of days, things felt strangely familiar, almost as if I never left. Bonds with old friends extend way beyond time and place, and coming home is a true reminder of who you are at your core, and of the people who will be in your life forever.

In many respects, coming home was by far the most difficult thing that I had to deal with on my Breakaway. It forced me to take stock, face the music and own the change that I had risked so much to enjoy. I would like to share some of my experiences with you so that you can at least understand logically how to prepare yourself for re-entering your previous life.

Decompress

Any activity that involves going into different environments with varied pressures requires some form of decompression. If scuba divers return to the surface of the water too quickly, they experience the bends; and if an aeroplane has an unexpected loss of cabin pressure, the whole structure could disintegrate.

Instead of going straight home at the end of my year, I had decided to spend some time with Emma in the United Kingdom. Our long-distance relationship, which started in the UK, and then blossomed while we were travelling in areas beyond our comfort zones, had to come full circle. Emma had done her bit to keep the relationship going by rendezvousing with me all over the world, so it felt right to go to the UK to be with her and to integrate myself back into what I called "reality".

I knew I had scratched the travel itch when I was sitting on a truly beautiful beach pining for my girlfriend and the hectic energy of the city – just to feel that I was getting back into the swing of life. I felt so hungry to take my career forward that I just threw myself into the thick of things without truly acknowledging the necessary period of decompression. Even though London is one of the world's greatest financial and cultural centres, and a place in which I had spent a significant amount of time, it was far from "my reality".

I arrived in London with limited financial reserves, lived under Emma's roof and relied on a small amount of money with which to enjoy one of the most expensive cities in the world. Even though I had committed to working on my book, I was unable to find part-time employment because of visa restrictions. I had hoped to be able to bring in some extra money and enjoy the summer with Emma and all of her friends, who were quietly evaluating me, the mysterious vaga-bond. Many of her contemporaries were married with kids and were in very stable positions, so we often dined in establishments that caused me to break into a sweat as I read the prices on the menu.

Decompression involves the need to release the pressure that results from the need to feel accepted, comfortable and in sync with your environment. In London, I was very much out of tempo with all the things that people associate with the place. Even though I was keen to become a bit more upbeat, moving from the often easygoing pace of a

Breakaway, to the hectic streets of the UK's capital, was completely overwhelming.

While most of my friends were climbing the corporate ladder at an alarming speed and enjoying massive salaries in their early 30s, I was still unclear about where I was going to take my career and was busy evaluating a number of different ideas I had unearthed on my trip: this book was one of them.

The reality is that no matter how much you try to remind yourself that your contemporaries truly envy the Breakaway experience you have just enjoyed, you may find yourself – in light of your financial insecurity and lack of real traction in your career – wanting what they have.

Remember, it takes real guts to step off the conventional path that many of your friends walk almost unconsciously. It is natural for you to start comparing yourself to your friends. You cannot fight millions of years of evolutionary instinct that will encourage you to emulate your tribe as a way of feeling accepted. Allow those emotions to take their course and focus on your new journey.

You will also find that you lost touch with a lot of people during your Breakaway. When the initial excitement of your return fades, you might notice that even some of your good friends have forgotten about you. Having been out of sight and mind for so long, getting yourself back into social consciousness takes a great deal of work. I often had to remind some of my best friends in London that I was still in town. This reality of feeling slightly forgotten only added to the pressure of returning to a place that I would usually call my second home.

There was no question that many of my friends still held a deep affection for me and considered me very much an integral part of their crew, but things had changed. School and university groups had been broken up by distance, marriage, babies and time. You may return home to find that the clusters of people who formed the core of your friendship group have been scattered.

It is human nature to compare ourselves and to want to be accepted by our peers. I found that my lack of grounding, stability and direction, which was a perfectly normal way of being on a Breakaway, was being tested to the limit as I felt compelled to integrate into an environment that was not actually my own,

I found myself overwhelmed by stress and pressure and started to question whether my Breakaway experience had ultimately been a valuable experience, or something that just got me more lost than I had been before.

Be grateful for the whole experience

You will return home with a new sense of your vocation, or perhaps several options that you are still evaluating. When you have poured your heart and soul into a new career or business opportunity, it is very easy to begin assessing the success of your Breakaway on the realisation of that opportunity.

Avoid trying to limit the success of the experience to one thing. In my case it was this book, which was the most exciting and personal of my creations. At times, I found myself basing the whole value of my Breakaway experience on whether I would ever get it published. But, you have no idea how all of the experiences you have enjoyed will crystallise into the vocation that will ultimately give your career the structure and certainty that you seek.

What made my post-Breakaway period easier was expanding my mind and acknowledging how many ways it had benefited me. I spent days looking at all the photos, reliving amazing moments in my mind, and reflecting on how every experience had shaped my character, world view, emotional resilience, and overall network, while creating memories and amazing relationships.

The world changes so quickly that any exciting career or business opportunity could become irrelevant to you or the market quicker than you realise. Your ability to effectively respond to this reality is the true gold that you will discover within yourself during a Breakaway. Adaptability, resilience and open-mindedness are all necessary skills when we step off the beaten track and our expectations are suddenly not met. Be sure to take time to reflect on all aspects of your experience that lie beyond the vocation.

Go full circle

One of the reasons why I struggled so much in London was because I had not yet gone full circle. We may all be citizens of the world, but home is one of the most fundamental ways of grounding ourselves. After about 18 months away from South Africa, I started to feel that the very fabric of my being was being unstitched and that I was floating away.

A Breakaway is a temporary upheaval of the roots that ground a person. Our deepest connections to our family, friends and culture stay intact, but when we have been away for longer than expected, these also start to loosen, which can have a profound impact on the psyche.

What's more, you cannot fully comprehend the change you have experienced until you have gone full circle. Our life decisions are based on expectations of how a career, relationship or place will fulfill our values. The fundamental wisdom of a Breakaway is that it allows us to make decisions based on comparative experience. Touching base with all the aspects of your previous life will bring alive your new values or reinforce what is most important to you.

Be sure to get home. See your family, catch up with friends, re-engage with your old work colleagues, and go back to the office to see how it feels. Do this slowly, in increments, and focus on the most important areas first.

Do not focus on the money

There is a good chance that you would have sacrificed a good deal of your financial stability in order to get the most out of your experience. In other words, you might be broke. Not everyone is able to fully finance their Breakaway experience based on short-term vocational projects during their travels. Many people seek to open themselves to full exploration, which means not drawing on old skills that could be used to make money.

It is important to remind yourself why you completed the Break-away in the first place. You made a conscious decision to sacrifice the momentum in your career to explore and gain more experience. The gains you have made in self-awareness, broadened perspective and ultimately your capability for innovation, are far more valuable in the long term than the money in your bank right now.

Do not become overwhelmed by complexity or the need to make a decision.

When you open yourself up to so much opportunity, it is only normal that you will be sitting with several potential vocations and perhaps a stream of ideas related to each. When you come back, you could feel that your window of experience is closed and that it's about time you made the decision about which vocation will take you forward. You may also be under pressure from those that you love who are reliant on you for financial security and emotional stability. This brings significant pressure, because ultimately you don't want to make the wrong decision and put years of energy and lots of money into the wrong one.

You might polarise between ideas that were very exciting but still very theoretical, and ideas that really will get the bank balance ticking over but which were not one of your long-term vocational journeys. The first thing you need to accept is that fresh from your return, your ability to make decisions that have long term implications is ultimately impaired. Remember to carry on the process you developed during your Breakaway. Give yourself the financial freedom to continue your incremental process of gaining more experience and allowing the decisions that influence your vocation to shape themselves.

Own your new values

You have gone on your Breakaway to discover more about yourself and to let go of the things that were holding you back. Every relationship, organisation and even community has a set of values, beliefs and identity that become entrenched over time. On our Breakaways we often assume that by having had an experience and having accessed a whole new way of being, that we are transformed. Then we return home and before long we have slipped back into the same patterns, routines and cliques that we were trying to escape from in the first place. Cultures are powerful things and can easily swallow and assimilate any new change that you would want to bring into your life.

After I was picked up from the airport by my mother, and the tears of joy had run their course, I slowly returned to where I had left off with her in Columbia. It had been months since my vision on the ayahuasca had shown me the difficult truths of our relationship. Returning home, I was confronted by an even more fragile person who was no doubt relieved to see the return of her main emotional crutch, her pillar of support. I should have introduced new boundaries that protected me from the harmful realities of her addiction while allowing her to take responsibility for her own life. Instead, I witnessed a further regression of her physical, emotional and financial stability, and I jumped straight back in to try to get her right.

After a couple of months, I invited Emma to come and spend some time with me in South Africa. Considering my difficult financial position, a botched decompression and a real need to get home, I had left London full of doubt, not only about our relationship, but also about my future. With so many insecurities raising their heads at the same time, it had been very difficult for me to differentiate between them.

I am so grateful to Emma. She was brave enough and had enough love for me to give up her family, friends and stability to move to Cape Town. She made the move despite the fact that I was still very fragile after the conscious unravelling of my Breakaway. I was really hoping that things would come together for me. I had finally returned home and had the opportunity to settle and to build the structures that would make my Breakaway worthwhile.

Emma joined me for what would be the culmination of my Breakaway – the climax of my story. At the time, I was not aware that my vision on ayahuasca that had opened my eyes to the reality of my mother's situation, had not been about final acceptance. Rather, it had pulled away the veil of denial that had protected me from the difficult realities of my past and the sadness of her condition.

Finally, my true anger, fear and impotent rage had a chance to air themselves for the first time, and I found myself having to cope with unprecedented emotional upheaval. Rather than establishing proper boundaries with my mother and seeking professional support, my pain was too great and I slipped back into the well-grooved pattern of denial and trying to help her. I did all of this while trying to re-establish my own life and be in a relationship with Emma. I needed to hold the space for her to settle herself, too.

This would culminate in a complete breakdown. I became ill for a month and, for the first time in my life, I was depressed. That time almost saw the complete disintegration of my relationship with Emma. It was not what I had envisioned for the culmination of my trip, but my breakdown, as painful as it was, ultimately paved the way for my real Breakaway.

I believe that Breakaways are about freedom. By exploring other careers and ways of living, we are given the opportunity to choose more fulfilling options for us. Only by letting go of the expectations that we are entitled to both happiness and success by following convention and relying on other people, can we adapt and find our own paths. By appreciating the situations over which we have no power, we gain the greatest freedom by embracing our ability to choose our own meaning. We can choose not to be victims and to use our experiences to make a difference.

My real learning would be understanding where the locus of control to choose really lay. This was where my final Breakaway journey would take me: my childhood. For many years I had denied my true feelings – first through things outside of myself, like drugs and alcohol, then through the complicated mechanism of the mind, which allowed me to rationalise, avoid and plan my way out of confrontations with my true emotions.

Even though I maintained an illusion of control, the unconscious denial of my deepest wounds made me a prisoner to my past. The experiences of Vipassana and Ayahuasca had given me an insight into the depths of my unconscious and an awareness of how dominant these forces could be in my life. Finally, I had to process them consciously.

With the help of an amazing counsellor, I was able to confront the last layer of the onion. Dredging through the mud of my childhood was the most difficult experience of my life. Going back to those dark times and embracing unadulterated, irrational pain, I was no longer denying, weighing up or making excuses. I was touching the raw nerve of my experiences as a young boy.

Acceptance is an emotional process, not a logical one. For years, I had thought that the process of coming to terms with something was about shifting one's perspective, being grateful and trying to understand the logical reason for why things took place. I had become very good at using sophisticated window-dressing to glamourise a house that had its foundations on unstable ground.

For many years I had also told myself that I had let things go, yet everything about my actions suggested that I was still responding to life from the frame of reference of my difficult youth. Many people believe that it is not good to dig up the past and that one should just let things go. I totally agree – but only when one has confronted raw experiences and allowed the emotional wounds to heal themselves. This is the only thing that brings true acceptance of one's past.

I would discover that this process of acceptance ultimately brings not only forgiveness for one's self and for others, but also gratitude for even our darkest experiences. I would discover that I had my mother to thank for all of my qualities that I now hold dear.

I would also learn that the skills that I valued most in myself were borne of the difficult situations to which I had been forced to adapt as a child. I had become a pretty good influencer, storyteller and ulti-mately, a speaker, in order to convince myself and others that I was okay. But in many respects, I was still deeply unhappy. To protect my addiction, I developed superior skills as an actor. An ability to project and share ideas with people would become one of my greatest assets, but it was borne from my most difficult situations.

The loss of my father, which was ultimately very sad, gave me the freedom to explore other career paths. His significant hold on my life values became looser in death. His battle with cancer from an early age had given me the opportunity to question how I valued success, and to prioritise the things that would ultimately give my life meaning.

My most difficult life experiences had given me my vocation: that of a coach. Having consistently tried to heal my mother, it was only natural that I would take on a profession geared towards personal change and transformation.

The word "vocation" essentially means a calling to be of service to other people. I would come to realise that this calling would not come through a degree or some kind of certification from a university, but rather through a holistic culmination of all of my life experiences. The true freedom of my Breakaway was the understanding and appreciation of why we are relationship with things around us – from families to intimate partners, friends and work.

I could not love my mother for who she is until I had accepted how she chose to live her life. I could never give unconditional love to Emma until I had let go of the warped conditions in which I had felt loved in my childhood. I could never be a good coach until I was fully able to accept the choices of my clients and their own unique journeys. I could never be fulfilled by my work until what I gained from it went beyond satisfying my own insecurities.

The current economy provides so much opportunity and places so much emphasis on expressing a sense of meaning through the work that we do, so we have to be very clear about the ultimate drive that underpins our work. If my need to coach was based on the ultimate need to heal my mother, I would never be fulfilled in my work – that would be something I could never do. If your desire to follow a career path is to gain the acceptance of your peers, you will never have that acceptance, because until you can accept yourself and your own journey, no career or friend will be able to anchor off you.

The people who are ultimately free of the need to fulfill themselves through the work that they do are truly of service to their customers. They adapt more quickly to the needs of the market because they are not attached to old ideas of themselves or of their products. They provide better customer service because they are genuinely concerned with meeting the needs of customers, and not satisfying their egos or bank balances. They are better leaders because they can embrace the unique journey of each individual they lead.

When all of the great spiritual cultures talk of enlightenment, they speak of the ability to understand one's true nature and to be free from anything that prevents one from practising unconditional love and acceptance of one's self and others. I was a long way off from this reality, but my Breakaway opened my eyes to the freedom of which the great sages speak.

My true nature as an expression of life is change. Life is not fixed, rigid or constrained. It is filled with diversity and surprise. Those unexpected turns do offer both joy and sadness, but the misery we endure is based on our inability to face up to both our biggest wounds and greatest aspirations, to honour them and step into new potential for ourselves.

Remember, as we gain and lose in this game of life, nothing should be taken personally, or we will become victims. In our own weird little ways, we are all doing the best with what we are given.

* * *

I remember being five years old. We were on holiday together as a family. My father took me out into the waves and pushed me in on a small bodyboard. Mom and my younger brother, Jake, were sitting on the beach, watching enthusiastically. As we waited for the waves, we spent time together, just the two of us, talking and then embracing the rhythmic silence of the ocean. I was in a womb that represented safety, nurturing and love.

As a wave approached, my heart raced and I let out screams of fear as I prepared myself for the push into the oncoming swell. Feeling my father's presence and his arms around me, I felt safe in the now unpredictable realm.

Off I went, and as I washed up on to the shore, grinning from ear to ear to the wild jubilation of my mother, I remember feeling so happy and so held.

I would have to go on my own journey on this wild wave that we call life. Despite storms clouding the love that my family shared, it was always there. Despite the confusion and complexity of finding one's purpose in life, our vocation is always there. We just need to embrace all that makes us unique and have the courage to follow it. Sometimes we need to Breakaway to discover it and sometimes we need to embark on a journey to realise that it was there all along.

I came from the depths of this collective expanse
I remember the stillness, the calm, the protection!
I know not of what karmic swells sent me upward to the realm of
the surface, but it has been my world ever since.

My journey began just as others had ended. The voice of the creator
came howling across the surface, singing its synchronous tune,
calling us to duty from the depths!

Many before me came from calmer beginnings, but my ripple was borne from the passionate collision of swells gone before.

To honour them, I wanted to rise, to touch the heavens and to crash with such power that I would be remembered long after sinking into sand on distant shores.

Where was I going? I do not know! I had heard of far-off beaches filled with rugged beauty and colourful rainbows.

The liquid surface however, gave no hint of destination, ever changing, sometimes calm, sometimes stormy.

Racing along under a quiet night's sky, feeling alone, feeling lost, where was I to find purpose and destiny? The moon and stars were not forthcoming, nor the great beasts.

Then, finally, there it was the one, the only the blue!

With it came the vision, the connection and the guidance. It had

been there all along.

I just needed to look inward, the one, the only, the blue!

So, as I sign off from this Breakaway journal, I am preparing for my next adventure. This book is a gift and innovation that my experience gave me, which I now have to take to the world. My sense of vocation as a coach has been renewed, and I have never felt more inspired to guide people on their Breakaways and vocational journeys in general.

I am preparing myself for one of my biggest adventures yet – a committed relationship with my girlfriend, Emma – another treasure I discovered on my trip. My relationship with my mother has never been better, thanks to the detachment of the warped strings that tied me to co-dependency. I feel that I have a far richer sense of myself and the world. As you embark on your own voyage, I wish you all the best!

Godspeed!

Acknowledgements

My family is a melting pot of chaos, charisma and love. Without them, I would not be the person I am today. My Breakaway journey was enriched by my girlfriend, Emma, whose love and compassion has lead me to blossom in ways that I would never have predicted and whose skills as an editor and proofreader cannot be appreciated enough.

My first big Breakaway would never have happened without the fellowships of AA and NA, nor the generosity of spirit of Clive Sher, Jim Devlin, Mark Emmerich and my first mentor, Mark Dodsworth. I would also like to convey my love to my surrogate parents, Ann Crotty, Bridget Rosholt and Georgina Relly. I am also thankful for the amazing support of Ira Epstein, who performed the thankless task of managing my education and early career development in the absence of my father.

I would like to acknowledge my editor Michelle Bovey-Wood for holding my hand through the first book and doing a truly excellent job in polishing this piece. Vanessa Wilson and the rest of the team at Quickfox Publishing allowed me to self-publish this book with professional expertise. Thanks to all of my proofreaders.

To all the people who piloted this book, most specially Helena Wedgewood, Hamish Mackay Lewis and George Eadie, thanks for your crucial feedback that sculpted the final manuscript.

This book would not have been possible without all the people who helped me fund the publishing. Thanks again to Patrick Schofield and his team at Africa's premier crowdfunding platform, Thundafund, for giving me the means and guidance to rally their support.

My heart also goes out to all the amazing people around the world that I met on my Breakaway. Your generosity truly transformed my appreciation of humanity.

We all stand on the shoulders of giants and it is in this spirit that I would like acknowledge all the pioneers of personal development, creativity, eco-psychology, entrepreneurship and spirituality who all contributed to the development of this book.

About the author

Jeremy Behrmann is a South African born speaker, coach and facilitator of global learning journeys. He has a masters in Economics and Business Studies from Edinburgh University and has globally-recognized certifications in coaching, entrepreneurship, wilderness guiding and creative problem-solving. He works with schools, professionals, corporate organisations and parents. He travels globally and lives in Cape Town.

To learn about the coaching, seminars and Breakaway experiences that Jeremy facilitates all around the world go to
www.elixirgroup.co.za